Using Networking and Communications Software in Business

Using Networking and Communications Software in Business

P.K. McBride

HEINEMANN
NEW·TECH

Heinemann Newtech
An imprint of Heinemann Professional Publishing Ltd
Halley Court, Jordan Hill, Oxford, OX2 8EJ

OXFORD   LONDON   MELBOURNE   AUCKLAND   SINGAPORE
IBADAN   NAIROBI   GABORONE   KINGSTON

First Published 1989

© P. K. McBride 1989

British Library Cataloguing in Publication Data
A CIP catalogue record for this book is available from the British Library

ISBN 0 434 91274 3

Produced by SC&E Morris Computer Services, Bodenham, Hereford

Printed and bound in Great Britain by
L R Printing Services Ltd, West Sussex

Contents

Introduction 9

Networks

Chapter 1 Communication within the Office 13

    What Makes up a Network? 14
    Other Networking Essentials 16

Chapter 2 Networked or Separate? 19

    The Networked Office 23
    Bigger Systems, Bigger Savings 25
    Hidden Costs? 26
    Cost Benefit Summary 27

Chapter 3 The Varieties of Networks 29

    The Background 30
    The Nature of Networks 31
    Coping with Collisions 40

Chapter 4 Networking Standards 43

    The OSI Model 44
    The IEEE Standards 46
    Non-Technical Summary 47

Chapter 5 Network Software 49

    Installation 49
    In Use 51
    The NETBIOS System 52
    The Network Commands 53
    Summary 64

Contents

Planning a Networked System

Chapter 6 Analysing Your Requirements   69

    Applications Programs   71
    Users and Workstations   74
    Printers and Print Servers   76
    Data Storage Requirements   77

Chapter 7 Hardware for the Network   81

    Dedicated File Servers   83
    The Sharing Workstation   84
    Back-up Systems   85
    Print Servers and Printers   86
    Netware   88
    Design for Reliability   88
    Typical costings   89

Chapter 8 The Office and the System   95

    Network Management   96

Installation and Management

Chapter 9 Installing the Network   101

    Stage 1 - The Trial Network   102
    Stage 2 - Applications Software   102
    Stage 3 - User Training   104
    Stage 4 - Cabling Up   104
    Maintenance and Trouble-Shooting   105

Chapter 10 Network Management   107

    The File Server   107
    Backing up files   109
    Managing the Print Server   110
    On Being a Network User   112

Networks and Application Software

Chapter 11 Sharing Data 115

    File and Record Locking 117
    The Deadly Embrace 118

Chapter 12 Suitable Software 121

    Database Management Systems 121
    Accounting Systems 122
    Spreadsheets 122
    Word Processing 123

Communications

Chapter 13 Electronic Memos
              and Networked Communications 129

    Mail, Memos and Calls 130
    File Transfer 131
    Calendars and Bulletin Boards 131

Chapter 14 Going On-Line 135

    Communications Basics 136
    Data Transmission 136
    Error Detection and Correction 138
    Terminal Emulation 140
    Other Facilities 140

Chapter 15 The On-line Services 143

    Electronic Mail 144
    Telex 146
    Direct Data Communications 147
    Internetworking 148
    Accessing the Databanks 148
    Other On-line Services 151

Contents

Appendices

Appendix A The Multi-user Alternative   157

    Time Sharing   158
    Downtime   159
    Reaching the Limits   160
    Pricing   160
    Operating Systems   161
    In the Office   162

Appendix B The Data Protection Act   165

    Registration   166
    Coverage and Exemptions   166
    The Data Protection Principles   167
    In Practical Terms   168
    Security   168
    Further Information   169

Appendix C SageNet   171

Appendix D Tapestry II   175

Appendix E Product Suppliers   177

Glossary   183

Index   189

Introduction

Until recently the cost of setting up a computer network has been too high for most smaller firms to contemplate. Now, low-cost but reliable PC's can be linked by low-cost and reliable networking hardware and software. If the computers are already there, it can cost as little as a few hundred pounds to link them into a working net. If there is a new computer system going in, or the existing one is to be extended, using a network could well save money, as hardware and software resources can be shared across a net. And, once in place, a network can make significant improvements to the efficiency of a business. Any firm which has more than one computer in the office should be thinking seriously about linking them together.

This book will set out to answer the key questions about networks in business. What are they and why should we bother with them? How can a network improve the firm's performance? Is it difficult or expensive to set one up properly and would it be worth the effort? What benefits are to be had from computer communications within the firm?

Introduction

This is a practical book, but practical in the sense of how networks and communications can be used within a working office, not of how they work at a detailed technical level. Where examples are needed, I have drawn most of them from SageSoft's new MainLan, a good mainstream product for a small to medium-sized commercial organisation, and from Torus Tapestry, a more sophisticated and considerably more costly system. Though they are by no means the only products on the market, they do show what can be done with high quality, user-friendly software.

Up until the last couple of years, networking was the preserve of the bigger, richer organisations, too expensive and complex for general use. As a result, it still tends to be swathed in jargon. There are LAN's and WAN's, baud rates and buses, broadband and baseband, CSMA/CD, IEEE and a whole mess of technical terms that the computer experts will throw at anyone who mentions networks. Fortunately, an awful lot of it is irrelevant to those people who just want to use them in their offices. This book tries to concentrate on the bits that matter.

There is a glossary of the more commonly used technical terms at the back of the book.

Networks

1

Communication within the Office

In this chapter we will look at the nature of networks, at what is involved in setting one up, at their potential for economies and improved efficiency in an office, and at some of those extra costs of networking that may not be apparent at first.

Put simply, a network is a set of computers, joined together by cable. Thus linked, they can communicate with each other, share printers and other peripherals and have access to a common set of program and data files. A network may be vast, encompassing hundreds of computers and spread across continents; it may link together mainframes, minicomputers and micros; its users may be a host of individual enthusiasts or firms; or the network may consist of no more than two machines, joined with the sole purpose of sharing a printer or hard disk.

The larger systems are generally referred to as Wide Area Networks or *WAN*'s. Some are run by single organisations, with perhaps the biggest being the world-wide network run by IBM for its own use, linking its many research establishments and sales organisations, so that scientists and managers in America, Europe, Australia and elsewhere can pool ideas and draw upon each other's expertise. Within the UK many of the leading chain stores and supermarkets have networks that span the whole country, with every store feeding data back to the central organisation.

Some wide area networks, like SEAQ, the Stock Exchange system, are not restricted to a single firm but are run as a service for interested individuals and businesses. This may be of little relevance to the general reader but there are other WAN's - principally the open access communications and database networks such as Telecom Gold - that are important and are well worth a look at.

The main focus in this book is upon networks within a firm, and within a single site, where the computers are never more than ten or twenty metres from each other. These are Local Area Networks or *LAN*'s, and from here on out the term network will mean Local Area Network unless it specifically says otherwise. These need not necessarily be small - you can join several hundred computers into such a network - but whatever the size, they have much in common. The main difference between a 4-computer network and one with 64 computers will be the impact on your bank balance.

Installing a network should not be seen as a once-and-for-all job that has to be fitted in full from the start, for they are dynamic systems, growing and changing throughout their life, in response to growth and change within the business. New computers can be brought in to extend the network or to replace old machines, at any time and usually with very little trouble. This flexibility is one of the most attractive features of networks and it also makes it possible for an organisation to test the waters with a very small network, adding onto it when it has proved its worth.

What Makes up a Network?

The most important components are, obviously, the computers. In a small business, these will normally be IBM or IBM-compatible PC XT's with perhaps a few of the higher-performance AT's. Larger firms, where greater speed or capacity may be needed, might include a minicomputer in the network. A design or engineering office may well have a network composed largely of high-resolution graphics terminals to run their CAD software, with a smattering of PC's for routine word processing and accounting.

That brings up an important point about a network; you can link different types of machines together. This is significant even if you do not have any need for specialist computers, as it means that you can add new models into a network of old computers.

Next come the peripherals: hard disk drives and tape streamers, printers and plotters, modems and mice. With a network, you will usually find that you need fewer peripherals than with the same number of separate computers, for each user will have access to every peripheral that is attached to the network. Instead of having, say, a 20 Megabyte hard disk drive on each of half a dozen machines, two 60 Megabyte drives could service them all, for each computer will be able to store its files on either of the networked drives. One high quality printer may be enough to satisfy the needs of a 4-computer office, which without the network would have found it difficult to function without one per machine.

Cables are then needed to create the physical links between the computers. There are several alternative types of cable, each with its own advantages and disadvantages. Normally, you will also need a network adaptor card to plug into each computer, though there are networking systems around that do not require these interface cards. No special hardware is needed to bring the peripherals into the network, as these will be part of it via the computers to which they are connected.

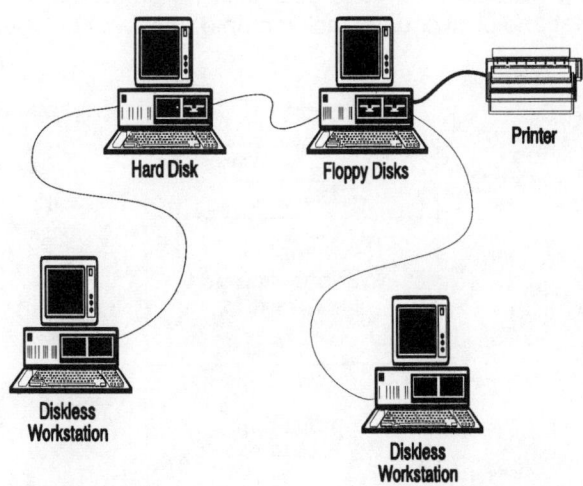

Figure 1.1 Peripherals can be shared on a network

Communication within the office

Cables and interface cards alone are not enough to make the net work; special networking software, or *netware*, is essential. This provides a means of identifying and addressing each component, and controls the flow of data around the system. When a file is sent to be printed, it is the netware that ensures that it reaches the right printer; when one computer user wants to access a file on another machine, it is the netware that makes this possible - or that prevents it. Security - the control of access to data - is an important function of the software.

Cable, adaptor cards and netware can be bought together in a total package - as are SageNet and MainLan. This is generally the simplest and most satisfactory way of setting up a net. Where no standard package will do the job, hardware and software can be acquired separately, though care has to be taken to ensure that they will work properly together. When the demands of an office outstrip the capabilities of an existing network, it should be possible to upgrade the network by replacing either the cable and cards or the netware. For example, a SageNet user who wanted the extra facilities of MainLan need only change the software. (Here the upgrade route is clear but a poor initial choice of network could leave you stranded, as you will see in the next chapter.)

Other Networking Essentials

If the network is to be put to its proper use, you will have to buy new applications software or upgrade your existing programs. Try to run an ordinary database or accounts package on a network and your data files

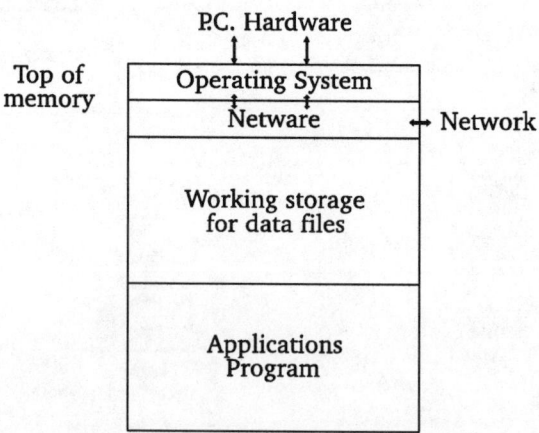

Figure 1.2 How the netware fits into memory

could get corrupted if two people attempted to update them at the same time. Your old single-user word-processing and spreadsheet software may work well enough - though getting printouts could be tricky - but you will have to be very careful about where and how you store the data files. Single-user software doesn't need to protect its data in the same way that multi-user software must. And Murphy's Law states that the files most likely to be corrupted are the ones that matter most.

You may also find that some newer and larger single-user programs will not run properly, simply because the networking software takes up memory that is needed by the application. Memory-resident 'pop-up' programs are also susceptible in this respect, for they tend to be stored in the same part of the memory. It doesn't mean that all your existing software will be made redundant by the net, but you will have to check it out carefully at first and it will be essential to take special steps to protect the integrity of your data.

Last, but by no means least, are the people who will use the network, for the system will be meaningless without them. They will need training, and some re-organisation of duties will be necessary. There must be a network manager, responsible for the smooth running of the net, its software and its data files. Other people in the office may also be put in charge of specific aspects of the system; at the most mundane level, whose job is it to make sure that there is paper in the printer?

2

Networked or Separate?

Having read this far, you might be starting to wonder whether or not networking is worth the effort and expense, so perhaps it is time to look at some positive aspects. A good way to do this would be to look at what goes on in the offices of a firm, before and after it installed a network.

C. Fairer & Sons are distributors of electronic equipment and rigging gear to the boat-building trade and to sailing enthusiasts. Before they began networking they had been using computers for some time, gradually extending the range of work performed on them, so that it included stock control, accounting, financial planning and word processing. In all they owned five computers, each with its own varied peripherals and each used mainly by one person for one set of functions.

Place/Uses	Storage	Printer	Function
Warehouse	20 Mb Hard	Dot Matrix	Stock Control
Sales	20 Mb Hard	Daisywheel	Recording Sales / Invoicing
Accounts	Twin Floppies	Dot Matrix	Purchases / Accounts Reports
Secretary	Twin Floppies	Laser	Word Processing / Brochures
M.D.	20 Mb Hard	None	Customer Records / Planning

Networked or Separate?

The computers were a mixture of IBM PC's and Amstrad 1512's and 1640's, purchased over a period of several years. The managing director had the only one with a colour monitor, which he said was essential for viewing his spreadsheet graphs. All three of the hard disk drives had surplus capacity, but floppy disks would have been unable to cope with some of the large files processed on these computers. The laser printer was a recent acquisition, and was mainly used with a desktop publishing package to produce promotional leaflets and price lists. The secretary's old daisywheel had been handed on to the sales office, who passed their dot matrix printer to accounts.

While the use of computers had certainly improved the efficiency of their business, this system still left some jobs to be done manually and it generated a number of irritating chores. The sales office had to work from stock lists that were printed out at the end of each month, so was not always up to date on either the price or availability of items. The stores clerk, in turn, had to update his files from delivery notes as the orders were filled. Occasionally, goods were sold that were out of stock and when that happened the stores clerk had to ring through to the sales office who then had to recontact the customer and explain.

The accountant and the managing director had to take their data from stores and sales in paper form, and either process it manually or re-key it into their own files as needed. They are both involved in various aspects of budgeting and financial planning, and use the same spreadsheet program. Before networking, if they wanted to use each other's files they had to copy them onto floppy disk and pass that across.

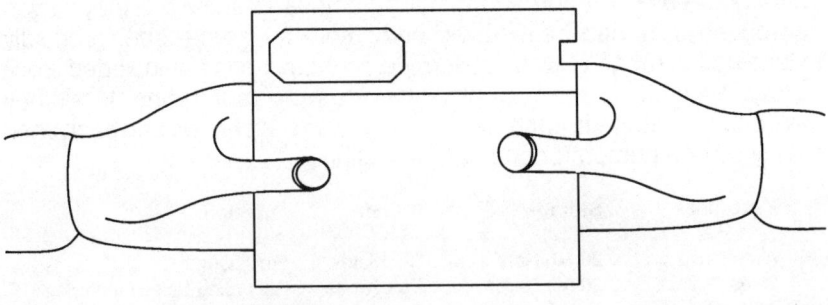

Figure 2.1 Data transfer?

Networked or Separate?

In the same way, the M.D. had to transfer to disk the files of customer names and addresses for the secretary to produce promotional mailshots; and the stores clerk would pass across the disks containing the stock descriptions and prices when she was putting together their brochures.

Most people were happy to use their own printers most of the time, but the secretary preferred her letters to be printed by a daisywheel rather than the laser printer, and the managing director could occasionally be seen wandering round the office with a disk in his hand, looking for an idle computer with a printer. (He could afford to buy one for himself but didn't want even more clutter in his office.)

The drive towards networking came from the accountant. Her files had grown to a size where a hard disk had become essential but she was aware that sales had spare capacity on their disk. She could also see that it would be much easier to produce the end of the month accounts if she could bring together the sales and purchase ledgers into a single system. The firm contemplated linking in stock control at the same time but, as there were some who were not totally convinced of the reliability of networking, it was decided that they should test the water with a limited system.

The first network was a two-station SageNet, linking the accounts and sales computers, with all files stored on the latter's hard disk. Its cost had been negligible; even with the additional expense of upgrading their accounting software to a networked version, the total outlay was less than that of a new hard disk. The system soon proved its value. There was less time wasted re-keying data, less effort needed to produce the end of the month accounts and less paper floating across the offices. What's more, as the accountant now had easy access to the sales data, she was able to monitor trends more closely and make better forecasts and recommendations for the future.

Satisfied by the trial, the firm decided to bring all of its machines into the network. For the secretary's and the M.D.'s computers, this could be done by buying off-the-shelf extension packs to the SageNet. Linking in the stock computer raised a couple of complications. As the warehouse was about 20 metres from the main offices an extra length cable would be needed, but that was only a matter of measuring up and ordering one to length.

File storage was the other problem. They needed to have the stock files on the same hard disk as the rest of the accounts data but there didn't

Networked or Separate?

seem to be a hard disk with much space to spare. At the time, the pattern of disk use was as shown here:

Device	Applications	Data	Spare
Stock Hard	8 Mb	7 Mb	5 Mb
Sales Hard	6 Mb	6 Mb	8 Mb
M.D. Hard	9 Mb	7 Mb	16 Mb
Floppies	8 Mb	5 Mb	N/A
Total	31 Mb	25 Mb	

Upgrading either the sales or the stock computer with a 40 Megabyte drive was one solution but there was another. When they looked at their total storage needs, they realised that there was a high degree of duplication of both applications programs and data. There were multiple copies of the accounting software, the spreadsheet and the word processor, and the managing director kept a copy of the accounts data. If they eliminated the duplication they would have room to store everything on the existing hard disks, including all the programs and data kept on floppies. (In practice, floppy disks would still be used - but only for back-up storage.)

Device	Applications	Data	Spare
Stock Hard	3 Mb	12 Mb	5 Mb
Sales Hard	14 Mb	2 Mb	4 Mb
M.D. Hard	6 Mb	8 Mb	18 Mb
Floppies	0 Mb	0 Mb	N/A
Total	23 Mb	22 Mb	

Though SageNet would enable them to centralise the accounts data, it has only limited disk-sharing facilities and would not allow them to run programs stored on remote disks. By opting for the more sophisticated MainLan netware, anyone using the network could run any applications wherever they were stored. In use, MainLan was almost identical to the SageNet, which they already knew well, and the existing cable and cards did not need to be replaced.

Some of the applications programs had to be upgraded to network versions and this, along with the hardware and netware, brought the total cost to a little over £1000. It was a significant investment but soon paid off in increased efficiency.

The Networked Office

Now that all stock and accounts files are stored on the same hard disk, and the accounting system is properly integrated, life is considerably easier for the stores, sales and accounts staff. Stock availability is checked automatically as invoices are written, and the stock records are updated by the system as the sales and purchases are processed. Though data is entered from three separate keyboards, it all reaches the same files and can be accessed from any computer on the network. The secretary can then draw directly from these when she comes to put together the price lists and sales brochures; and the managing director can keep his fingers on the pulse of the business without leaving his desk.

Figure 2.2 Data transfer!

With their word-processing, spreadsheet and database software all installed on a hard disk, anyone can run them from any computer - without the bother of having to find and load them from the floppy disks. As these are network versions, they have the added advantage of allowing several users simultaneous access to the data files. Thus, the accountant and the managing director can both be working on the same spreadsheet at the same time; the secretary can be drawing a mailing list from the customer database while the sales assistant adds the details of new customers. There is no question of having to wait for another person to finish with a file and pass the disk over, and no problem of creating alternative 'current' versions of what should be a single file.

Networked or Separate?

The network also allows people to print files on any of the printers. As long as everyone co-operates and makes sure that their local printer is switched on and loaded with paper, anyone can print anywhere at any time. It doesn't even matter if the printer is already in use, for the network runs a queuing system, so that if the printer is busy when a file is sent to it, that file will be put into temporary store on the print server, then run off later.

The secretary was the first to make use of this, as her laser printer was far too slow for routine letters, but the managing director also found it useful at a very early stage. He could send his spreadsheets and graphs to the dot matrix if he just wanted draft copies for reference, or to the laser printer for a high quality output. Printer sharing really showed its worth when the warehouse's old dot matrix finally gave up the ghost. They simply haven't bothered to replace it. Now that less data is being passed round on paper the firm as a whole has a lower printing requirement, and if the stores clerk does need to print stock summaries they are generally run off on the accounts printer, as this is cheap to use and quite fast enough.

The advantages of sharing data and resources became obvious at a very early stage; fewer peripherals meant fewer maintenance problems and lower running costs; sharing files meant that once data had been typed into the system, no-one was wasting time or creating errors by re-typing. These benefits had been anticipated; what was unexpected was the way that electronic mail improved communications within the business. The network's mail facility allowed users to send messages to each other's workstations, replacing memos and some of the internal 'phone calls. Unlike memos, electronic mail required no-one to deliver it, was instantaneous, was difficult to ignore and used far less paper - though sometimes people like to have printed copies of their mail. As a means of getting an answer to a question, mailing has proved to be as quick as a 'phone call and sometimes more convenient. Where neither party spends much time at their desk, getting in touch by 'phone can be a hit or miss operation, with several wasted calls in either direction. With electronic mail, the messages get through, whether or not there is anyone there to receive them. So, when the accountant sends a query down to the warehouse while the clerk is busy on the shelves, she will know that his reply will come through later when he returns to his desk - and she won't have to hang around waiting for it.

Some months into their use of the network the firm has discovered another significant benefit. When people had their own separate computers, they had been responsible for making their own back-up copies of programs and data files. Some had been less disciplined than others in this respect, and when problems did occur there were one or two nasty messes to sort out. When the network was installed, one (reliable) person was put in charge of backing up, and did so regularly and methodically. When a mains failure brought the system down one day the presence of up-to-date back-up copies of all files enabled everyone to pick up from more or less where they left off.

Bigger Systems, Bigger Savings

There would be little point in setting up a network simply so that you could share the odd peripheral - unless it was a particularly expensive article. The most commonly used pieces of equipment - good quality dot matrix printers and hard disk drives - cost roughly the same as the hardware and software needed to link two computers. In the example above, the savings on peripherals were not very significant. By networking, C. Fairer & Son were able to manage with one less printer and hard disk. Those hardware economies alone would not have covered the cost of the networking cable and interfaces. It was the improved efficiency through data sharing and mailing that made that system worth having.

There will be many situations were the hardware savings alone will justify the installation of a network. Take this instance of an advertising firm. Though not particularly large, it is spread over two floors of a building. It has half a dozen computers already in use, mainly for word processing, design and desktop publishing, with at least one person on each floor needing regular access to a laser printer. The quality outputs from this have proved to be invaluable in creating attractive proposals for potential clients, and are even being used as copy for newspaper advertisements.

With only one such machine in the building, it means that somebody is wasting far too much time running up or down stairs clutching a disk, and then hovering around the printer until it is free. The situation is clearly ridiculous and must be resolved. A second laser printer is the obvious answer but one with the required speed and quality could well cost over £3000. When the partners look at the position more closely, they see that a single printer can cope with the output demands; the problem lies in the inconvenience and time-wasting. If the computers were networked, the person at the distant workstation could send the file for printing and then collect the printed copy later, perhaps on the way past for coffee. A network suitable for this size and type of system would cost about half as much as a new printer and, as we saw earlier, will probably prove to have other beneficial side-effects.

Networked or Separate?

Go on to a larger office, supporting perhaps dozens of machines, and the hardware cost-savings start to mount up. There are, of course, no such savings if the peripherals are already in place and networking simply makes some of them redundant. But this situation would only exist with a static firm, working to a very restricted time-scale. Any forward-looking firm should be planning, if not for growth, then at least for the replacement of equipment over time. Networking can reduce future hardware requirements.

Hidden Costs?

In case all this sounds too good to be true, let's have a look at some of the less obvious costs that may be incurred on setting up a network.

For a start, the installation of the network may well run up expenses over and above the cost of the network hardware and software. A cable could be strung between adjacent desks without too much bother but if it has to cross walkways or go between different offices, or even different buildings, then it must be fitted securely. You may be faced with the expense of lifting floors, laying trunking or drilling through walls, and some disruption of the office while this is done.

Staff will need to be trained in the use of the new system, and there will no doubt be a few hiccups as people accustom themselves to new routines. With a user-friendly network, a few hours' formal training and a day's acclimatisation may be all that is necessary, but not all networks are user-friendly. Loss of work and increased overtime payments could be a significant expense if the system is large or complicated.

On anything other than a small network, you may have to invest in one or more high-performance computers to act as file servers. A network consisting purely of PC's may be fine, as long as the hard disk isn't too heavily used, but where files have to be accessed frequently the file server may become a bottleneck. This will be particularly true if the hard disk machine is also used as a normal workstation, for then it will be having to cope with the demands of the network and of the person at its keyboard. Just what constitutes 'heavy use' depends upon the nature and speed of the network, amongst other factors, and we will look at these more closely later.

As a rough rule of thumb, you could reasonably expect a normal PC to suffice as a file server on a network of up to 5 computers. As long as you avoided using programs which constantly accessed the hard disk it could also be used as a workstation. From 5 to 10, the PC should still be able to cope but only as a *dedicated* file server - that is, not used as a workstation. Above that point you will need to either bring in additional hard disks and have two or more file servers, or switch to a higher performance computer with a 286 or 386 chip, such as an IBM PC AT, one of the larger PS/2 computers or an Amstrad 2286 or 2386. Though faster than PC XT's, these can all use the same MS-DOS operating system and run the normal PC software, so the extra costs are purely in hardware.

You could run up against similar problems with print servers. If a file cannot be printed immediately it will be stored in a print queue on the server. For this to happen the network must have access to a floppy or hard disk at all times. If the print server is also used as a normal workstation, there could be conflict over disk access. Again, it is a matter of degree and will depend upon the patterns of use and the number of printers on the network. Where there are problems, a dedicated print server or the replacement of a floppy disk PC by a high-performance, hard disk machine may be needed.

Cost Benefit Summary

Costs

You must allow for:

- Networking hardware and software
- Upgrading software from single-user to network versions
- Training and practice time

You may need:

- Additional or replacement machines for servers
- Physical installation of cable

Benefits

You should enjoy a combination of:

- Hardware savings through shared printers and disk drives
- Software savings through shared programs
- Increased efficiency through data sharing
- Better internal communications
- Better control of data, with more reliable back-ups

3

The Varieties of Networks

Up to now, I have used the word 'networks' as if they were all much of a muchness. They aren't. You will find perhaps a wider variety of types, technologies, costs and ways of working here than anywhere else in today's computer field. Some networks use telephone-style cable, others co-axial or fibre optics; some have their computers connected in a line, others in a star or a ring; they vary in the speeds and the methods used for sending data from station to station, in the degree of control that they allow to users and in the ease with which they can be installed and used.

On the positive side, this variety does give potential customers a reasonable chance of finding something that will fit their requirements. Against that, it creates traps for the unwary, for some systems could well turn out to be expensive dead-ends when the time comes to extend or upgrade. Obviously there must be variety, for different organisations have different networking needs, but compatibility and connectivity are of paramount importance if a network is to have a long and useful life. This has been recognised by major manufacturers and customers, and the last few years have seen a very encouraging movement towards the establishment of common standards in networking hardware and software.

The Background

Ten years ago, the only significant networks in existence were ARCnet, a system designed by Datapoint for use with minicomputers, and IBM's Systems Network Architecture (usually abbreviated to SNA) which was built around mainframe computers and their terminals. This is still very much in use, and SNA-compatibility is a feature of some of the more sophisticated micro-based networks. It is worth remembering that ten years ago almost all 'serious' computing was performed on mainframes or micros. The PC had still to be designed and microcomputers had only just started to appear. Networking needs then were very different from those of today.

By 1980 the big computer companies, Xerox, Intel and DEC, had combined to produce a local area network system known as Ethernet. It was fast, efficient and reliable, and the design has withstood the passage of time to become the basis of one of the accepted standards. The original Ethernet is now widely used, as is a cut-down version, appropriately called 'Cheapernet', that uses thinner cable and a simplified wiring system.

The following year, Corvus Systems introduced their Omninet, a networking system that had been designed principally to share (expensive) hard disks among PC's. Omninet is still in use, and is the basis of Amstrad's new networking products.

About the same time, the Novell Corporation brought out their NetWare operating system for Ethernet networks. This fast and highly effective software has become something of a standard of comparison for all subsequent alternatives. A notable feature of Novell's Netware is that it imposes its own method of operation on hard disks, giving greatly improved performance.

IBM was rather slow off the mark in developing networking for PC's. It wasn't until 1983 that they announced their 'token ring' hardware, and even then it was only an announcement. The actual system did not appear for some time and the PC LAN software to run the ring was not produced until two years later. In between time, perhaps to maintain their presence in the new and growing market, they introduced their PC Network software, based on the MS-DOS operating system and designed for Ethernet-style networks, not the token ring.

The essential concepts behind networking are now well established, so it is scarcely surprising that recent years have seen no major new technical developments in this area. Low-cost products have appeared and have steadily improved in quality, with the best now comparable in performance to Ethernet-based systems. In commercial terms, Sage's new Lancia chip - nicknamed 'the network on a chip' - may prove to be the most significant new product, for this will enable manufacturers to build networking capability into their computers for only a few pounds. The other main area of advance has been in making networks more user-friendly: an essential development if they are to fit comfortably into a normal office environment.

The Nature of Networks

Throughout this time there have been a number of different strands of development, most significantly in the physical layout of networks: their *topology*, the type of cable used, the manner in which data transfer is handled and their presentation to the user. Though some of these differences are only really meaningful to a technical specialist, anyone considering setting up a network should at least be aware of them.

Traffic refers to the transmission of data across the network. The level of traffic obviously depends upon the number of computers but is also affected by the type of software being used. Databases tend to generate heavy traffic because the data files on the main hard disk are constantly being accessed by the users. Word processing and spreadsheets create little traffic as most of the operations are performed on data held in the local computer's memory.

Data collisions may occur when two computers attempt to gain access to the network at the same time.

Various *protocols* - low-level software routines - have been devised to deal with this problem and other aspects of data management.

In a *baseband* system the electrical signals are transmitted at their original frequencies on a single channel. It is similar to the way that signals are sent down a telephone line, although telephony is actually based on a different technology.

The Varieties of Networks

In a *broadband* system the transmissions are on several frequencies and so can carry audio, video and data simultaneously, in the same way that a TV or radio aerial lead can handle the signals for umpteen channels.

Topology

This term, borrowed from mathematics, refers to the way in which links are made between the nodes of a network. There are currently five topologies in general use in PC networks.

The *bus* structure has a central spine, with arms or *taps* extending off this to the nodes. Data travels in both directions along the spine, which must therefore consist either of a single bi-directional cable or a pair of cables. If a computer is sending data to another machine to the right, but the traffic flow is to the left, this creates no problems. The data will reach its destination on the return journey. Each station keeps a constant check on the traffic and picks off any data intended for itself.

Ethernet uses the bus structure. There the spine is a heavy co-axial cable, and each thinner tap cable is joined to it via a special piece of hardware called a *transceiver*.

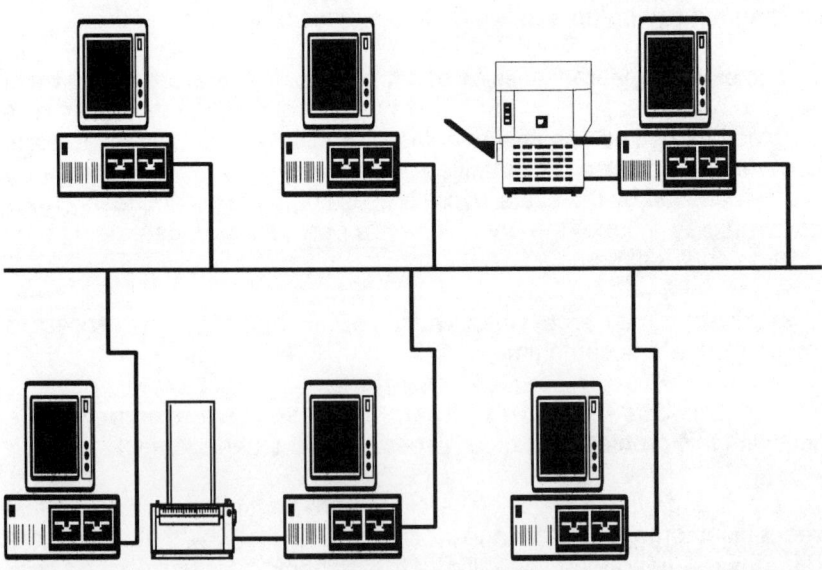

Figure 3.1 Bus topology

32

The Varieties of Networks

The *daisy chain* system is very similar to the bus in many respects. Here each station is joined to the next by a separate loop of cable, though the whole forms a single line. Normally the network interface or adaptor cards are designed so that data can pass from one link of the cable to the next, whether or not their host computers are turned on. When the traffic meets either end of the cable, a special end plug will reverse its direction of travel.

In practice a daisy chain is generally easier to set up than a bus. Most reasonably competent people can fit adaptor cards and plug in cables but wiring in transceivers calls for more skill and knowledge. The absence of this particular piece of hardware also tends to reduce costs on a daisy chain, though a bus structure may prove to be more economical on cable.

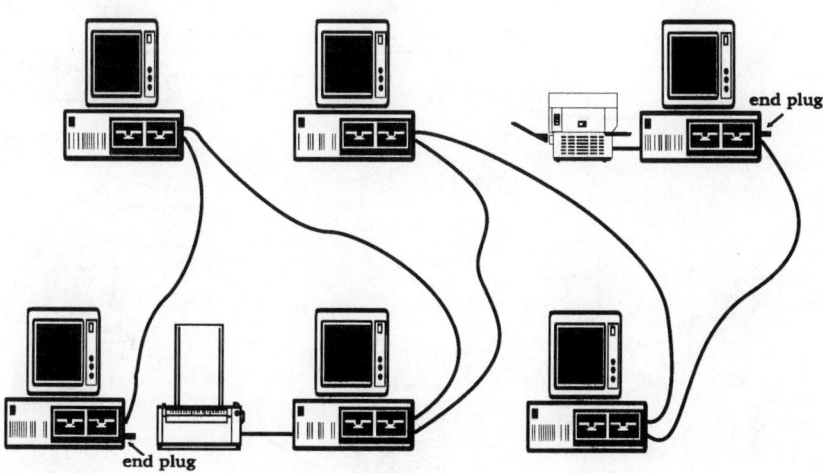

Figure 3.2 A daisy chain network

In a *ring* topology the two ends of the network are joined together, so that data is able to travel in a single direction all the time. This allows for higher speeds of data transfer and reduces the potential for collisions. (As we shall see shortly, data collision is a problem that all networks have to solve.)

Rings are not as flexible as the single line bus or daisy chain, and are not much used in PC networks.

The Varieties of Networks

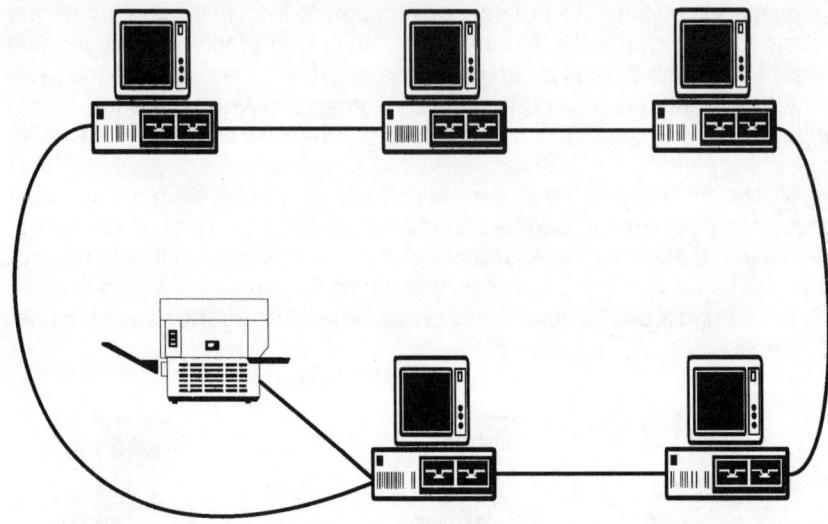

Figure 3.3 Ring topology

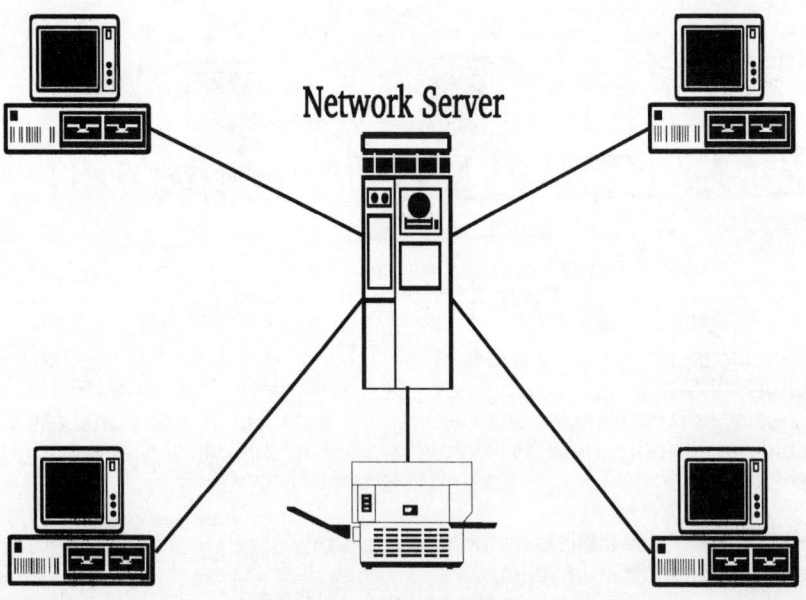

Figure 3.4 Star topology

The *Star* topology is the natural choice in multi-user systems, where there are dumb terminals linked into a central mainframe or mini computer and all sharing its processing power (see Appendix A). In PC networks, the hub is not a computer but a high-speed junction box whose sole purpose is to route data in the right directions. An example of these is the EPABX (Electronic Private Automatic Branch Exchange) system, which uses telephone technology in its switching. The weakness of the star topology is the obvious one; if the hub fails, the whole system is unusable. With a bus, daisy chain or ring, a non-functioning element can be bypassed quite simply, allowing the rest of the network to work normally.

The *token ring* is an interesting system, for it is one that works as a ring but is configured as a star. Its computers are connected by a dual cable to a central hub but data travels right round the system, just as if the nodes were connected in a ring. So, when computer A sends data to C it takes the route hub-B-hub-C. If a reply was sent, it would travel through hub-D-hub-E-hub-A (Figure 3.5).

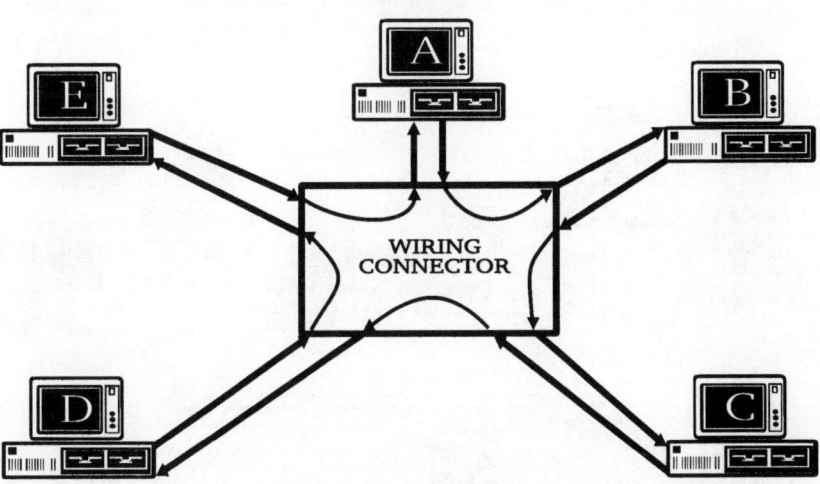

Figure 3.5 The token ring

Running the ring through a hub has the advantage of making it simpler to cope with the failure of individual stations. Should this happen, a bypass mechanism cuts the defunct machine out of the ring and restores connections to the rest. If, in our example, B failed, the route from A to C

The Varieties of Networks

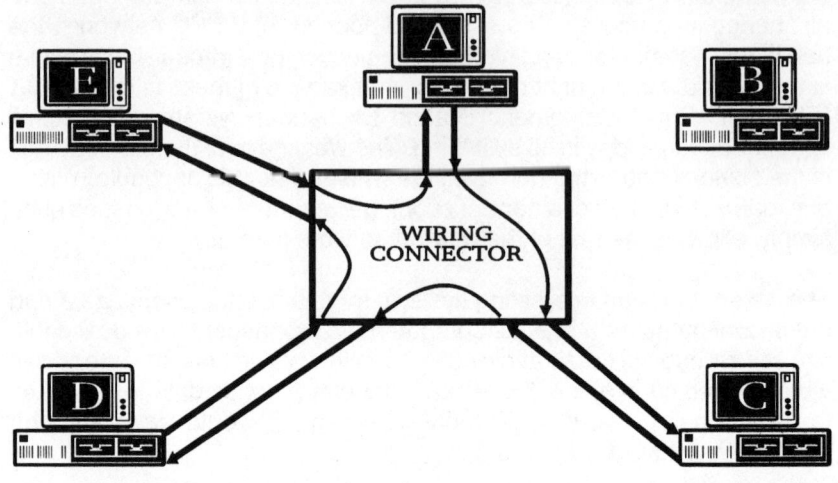

Figure 3.6 Bypassing a failed station

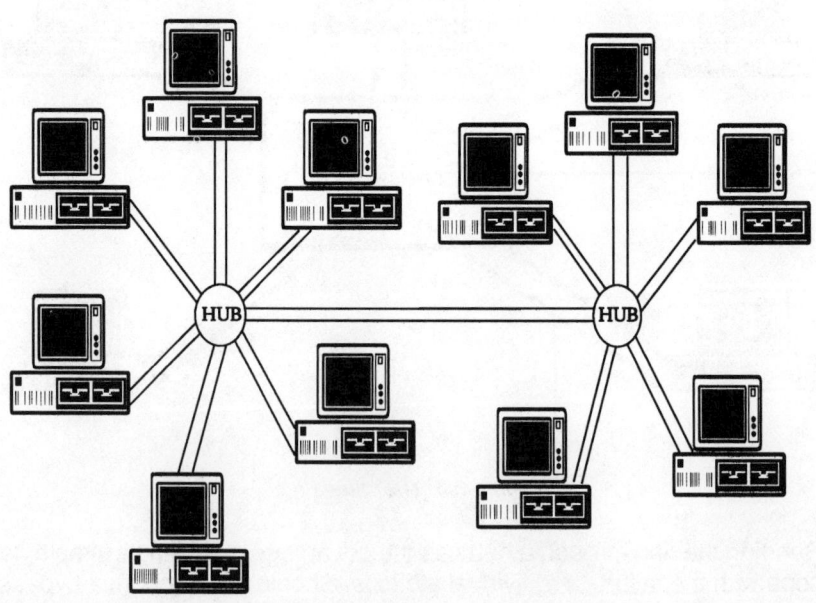

Figure 3.7 Linked token rings

The Varieties of Networks

would be through the bypass in the hub. However, as with a normal star, the whole system is only as reliable as the wiring connector at that hub.

In the IBM token ring, each wiring connector can manage up to eight stations, each no more than 100 metres away. For larger networks, the hubs are cabled together so that the ring runs round all of the connected stations. Such a system could bring together all of the computers in a large office block, with one or more stars on each floor. A particular advantage of the token ring, for IBM users, is that it is designed for easy connection to IBM mainframes and minis.

N.B. The *token* in the name refers to the method used to avoid collisions on the net. We shall return to this shortly.

Cables

Twisted pair cable is the cheapest and most commonly used type of networking cable. The simplest sort are almost identical to the old style telephone cables, consisting of a pair of copper wires; more often than not, though, there will be two pairs within the sheath. Normal twisted pair cable has only light insulation, so is thin and flexible and therefore quite easy to install, though it will need additional shielding in areas where there is a possibility of electromagnetic interference or physical damage. Signal quality deteriorates over distance, setting a maximum length of around 500 metres between the two ends of the network. This can be boosted to 1500 metres by the use of repeaters.

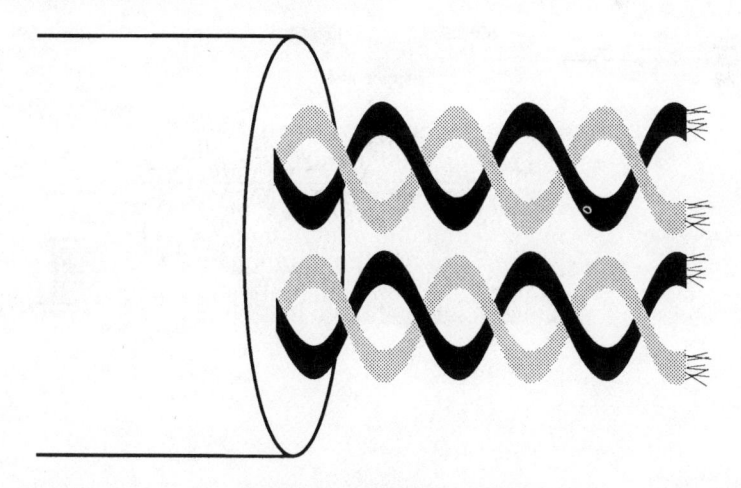

Figure 3.8 Twisted pair cable

The Varieties of Networks

A supposed advantage of twisted pair is that sometimes it may already be present in a building for an internal 'phone system. In practice, if it is there, it will rarely prove to be usable, either because the layout is wrong or the wiring is not of a high enough standard. Installing new cable is always the safest bet, and at around 60p per metre it adds little to the total cost of the system.

Shielded twisted pair is slightly heavier and more expensive, but gives better performance on large networks or where there is a problem of electrical noise.

Co-axial cable is the type used for TV aerials, with a central insulated copper core surrounded by a woven wire 'stocking'. It comes in two versions, thin and thick, with this latter being nearly 10mm in diameter.

It has a number of advantages over twisted pair, being less troubled by electromagnetic noise, capable of supporting higher speeds of data transfer and with a greater range. The thin coaxial can be used for networks up to 1000m in length; the thick up to almost 4000m. Both of these maxima can be increased threefold with the use of repeaters. Co-axial is well suited to *broadband* transmissions, so a single cable can be used to carry audio, video and data traffic.

On the downside, co-axial is more expensive than twisted pair cable, and is more trouble to install. It doesn't bend as easily around tight corners, and needs to be well protected from physical damage.

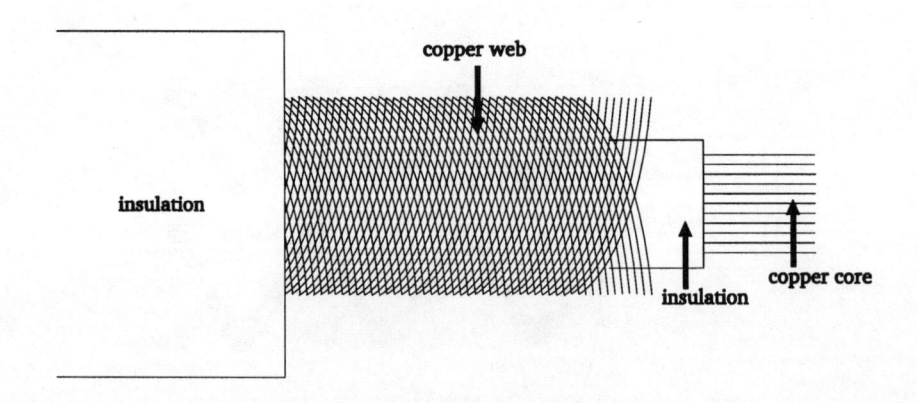

Figure 3.9 Co-axial cable

Optic fibre is the most costly of all networking cables and normally only used for very large installations, or those where its particular qualities are essential. As the fibres offer no resistance to the light signals that are transmitted along them, the cable allows extremely fast data transfer and distance is no object. Optic fibre cable can carry very high levels of traffic - audio and video as well as data. This is partly because you get an awful lot of fibres in a single slim cable, and each operates independently; and partly because the speeds are so high that, even with packet-switching, data is still getting through faster than through any form of copper wiring.

The medium is also very secure, in both senses of the word. It is secure from electrical interference - an important consideration in industrial installations or other places where there may be heavy electrical equipment - and it is secure from prying as it is so difficult to tap into. Indeed, making connections is always difficult, whether for the original network or to add new computers later, and installation is definitely a specialised job.

Where a network is to be used in a normal commercial environment, and only for data transfer between computers, a twisted pair baseband system will prove more than adequate for the job in the great majority of cases. The higher speeds of co-axial or optic fibre would only be needed where there are a lot of computers on the network or the nature of the office's work creates heavy data traffic.

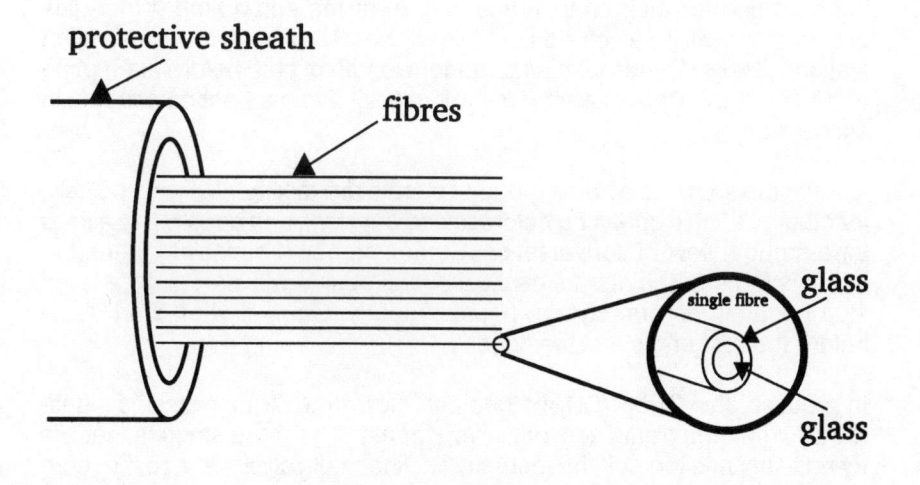

Figure 3.10 Optic fibre cable

Coping with Collisions

Whatever the nature of the network, it will only be able to transmit one item of data at a time. This doesn't mean that users will have to sit around twiddling their thumbs while one person accesses the hard disk. All networks chop up data streams into small packets and can handle several streams at once. It may look to the operators as if three of four people are all loading files simultaneously but what is actually happening is that a small fraction of each file is being sent to each user in turn. As networks operate far quicker than we do, the mere human on the other side of the keyboard is rarely aware of any delay. If transmissions are running at 4 Megabits per second (the speed of Sage's MainLan, for example), a single user could send a 50K file across the net in not much more than a tenth of a second. With five users sending 50K files, all five will still reach their destinations in under a second. Would you notice the difference?

All this, however, depends upon keeping the data packets separate, so that they do not corrupt each other. And most of all, that means preventing collisions.

The most widely used protocol for coping with collisions is *CSMA/CD*, which stands for Carrier Sense Multiple Access/Collision Detection. In this system, a transmitting station first checks the network for the presence of a carrier signal, which would indicate that the network was in use. If all is quiet, it sends its data. Now it may happen that two or more stations have been waiting for their chance and leap in at the same time. When this occurs there will be a collision but this will be detected by the transmitting stations. They will then wait for a random length of time before attempting to access the network again. This will usually avoid a second collision in succession.

It is just the same as when a group of people are talking. We wait, politely, for others to finish speaking before taking our turns and usually this allows for a smooth flow of conversation. Sometimes, and especially when the group is large or the debate hectic, several people will start at once, then stop because no-one can be heard properly. One will then start again before the rest and claim the floor.

In practice, the CSMA/CD method can slow down transmissions significantly when the traffic network is very heavy. The more stations that are trying to access the net, the more the likelihood of collisions, and the more time is spent in random waits.

The Varieties of Networks

Very similar to CSMA/CD is *CSMA/CA*, but here the solution is found in Collision Avoidance rather than detection. Stations check for the presence of a carrier signal and, if it is there, they wait for a random time before retrying. As before, the waiting time can result in noticeable delays where the traffic is heavy.

Token passing protocols take a very different approach to controlling access to the net. The idea behind these harks back to a system once used on some railways. Where up and down trains had to use the same single track - perhaps through a tunnel or along a branch line - it was vital that only one should be on it at a time. A metal ring, the *token*, would hang at the end of the track. If it was there when the train arrived the driver would take it, travel to the other end and leave the token there as he went by. If it was not present, the train would have to wait until it was brought back by another travelling in the opposite direction. It was a crude and inefficient system, but it did prevent collisions.

A rather more refined form of token passing is used on networks. Here the token is a signal that is passed around the network. When a station has possession of the token, it can attach a packet of data to it and transmit. If access to the network is not wanted, the token is passed on to the next station.

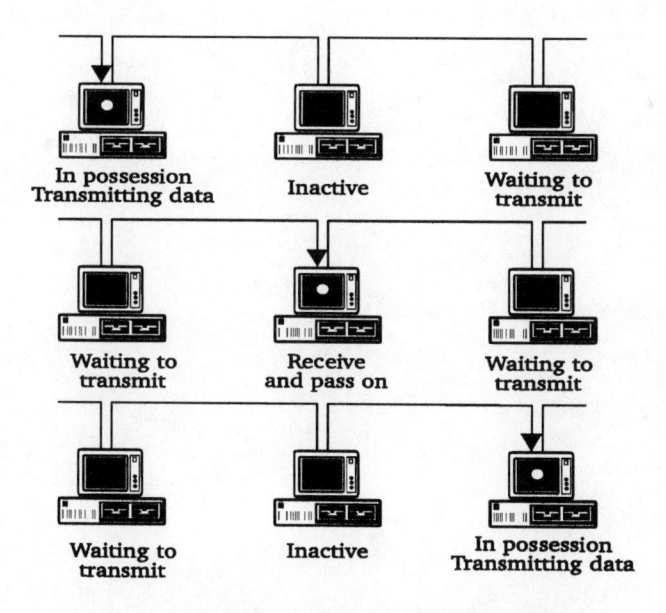

Figure 3.11 Passing the token

The Varieties of Networks

Theoretically, this method is more efficient than either collision detection or avoidance, especially where the network is under heavy use. There is no time wasted on repeated false starts and random waits as stations attempt to transmit. Against that, each station has to acknowledge and pass on the token, whether it wants to transmit or not. It cannot simply ignore what does not concern it, as on a CSMA/CD system. In practice, this means that a token-passing network with a large number of stations could have a lower working speed than that of an equivalent collision-detection network.

IBM's token ring is the best known network that uses this method but there are other token ring and token bus systems around.

4

Networking Standards

For the non-specialist, only two things are important about standards. The first is that they do exist; the second is that they do not really go far enough.

Two organisations are involved in establishing standards for networks. The International Standards Organisation (ISO), which has been working for some years on an Open Systems Interconnect model (OSI), and the Institute of Electronic and Electrical Engineers (IEEE), which has been producing specific standards for different types of network.

Standard setting is a complex business, and the process is further complicated by the need for consultation with and co-operation between manufacturers, consumers and government agencies, each with their own vested interests.

Networking Standards

The OSI Model

This should be seen as a theoretical framework within which network standards can be defined, rather than a set of standards. The concept behind the Open Systems approach is that network users should be able to incorporate the products of different manufacturers within a network, and that different networks should be able to link easily with each other. As the purpose of networking is to improve communications it is important that the networks themselves should not prove to be barriers to communication.

The OSI model divides networking into seven layers, rising up from the cables and other hardware to the applications programs that will run on networks. At the time of writing, only the bottom three have been defined in any detail, and for each of these the organisation has accepted a number of options, rather than establishing a single standard.

7	Applications	
6	Presentation	Applications level
5	Session	
4	Transport	
3	Network	
2	Data Link	Communications level
1	Physical	

Figure 4.1 The OSI layers

At the bottom is the *Physical* layer, covering cables and hardware interfaces, operating frequencies and other electrical aspects of transmission. A good example of a standard working at this level is the RS232 system. Almost all computers nowadays are fitted with an RS232 serial port, almost every serial printer has an RS232 connector and suitable leads can be obtained from just about every accessories supplier. Ethernet and the token ring (to IBM specifications) are both accepted as Layer 1 standards.

Layer 2 is the *Data Link*, concerned with the organisation of data packets and error checking at the lowest level. CSMA/CD and other protocols for collision management fall within the scope of this layer.

Networking Standards

The *Network* layer (3) defines methods of routing and relaying, and of attaching addresses to data packets so that they reach their intended destination. In practice, this is not needed on baseband systems except where there are links with other networks.

The physical, data link and network layers are all highly interdependent and are often grouped together under the heading *Communications* level.

At the *Transport* layer (4), we start to move away from the nitty gritty of the signals travelling round the network and begin to focus on how the network is used. This layer covers techniques for slicing data streams into packets for transmission, reassembling them on arrival and error handling at the user level. It aims to answer the question of how, having chopped a file into small chunks, do you ensure that all the pieces reach the other end and in the right order?

Layer 5 relates to *Session* management. When an application program requires a station to communicate with another, how is the session started and ended? Perhaps even more importantly, what happens if the communication session is interrupted part way through? Can the program recover from an interruption, and can the network recover?

IBM's NETBIOS has become the de facto standard for this layer, partly because it works very well, partly because it is IBM's. But it does mean that any NETBIOS-compatible software should be able to run safely on any NETBIOS-compatible network.

By the time you reach layer 6 - *Presentation* - the definition of standards is becoming rather hazy, though the need for standardisation is as great here as it is lower down. This layer relates to the display of data and the translation between those character sets used for display and for transmission. The good old ASCII code sets out a standard for handling (English) letters, digits and common symbols but foreign letters, block graphics, mathematical symbols and the other special characters that are included in the display capabilities of most computers are not covered by that code. Even more problematic is the translation of full graphic displays.

Fortunately, these are rarely problems from the user's point of view. The shortage of standards means that the software houses develop their own solutions, and we are able to get on with the job of using their products.

The final layer covers the *Applications* programs that are to run on networks. In an ideal world, all software would work in a similar fashion, so that when users transferred from one network to another they didn't have to learn how to use it all over again. At the most basic level it would help, wouldn't it, if the same function key always called up a Help screen, or if the Load/Save File menu could always be pulled down from the same corner of the screen?

The IEEE Standards

The Institute of Electrical and Electronic Engineers set up their 802 Standards Committee in 1981, with the aim of creating specifications that would allow different manufacturers to produce fully compatible equipment. These standards are not produced in isolation from commercial realities, and all of those seen so far have been heavily dependent upon one or other existing network. Three are particularly worth noting.

IEEE 802.3 - CSMA/CD Systems

The 802.3 standard is the most significant one for those of us interested in PC networks. Sometimes referred to as 'Ethernet', it is based upon the later version of this network (though the original Ethernet is not compatible with 802.3 products). Like the other IEEE standards, this is only concerned with the communications aspects of networks - layers 1 to 3 in the OSI model.

The initial 802.3 standard required that the network should be a baseband system running at 10 Megabits per second. There have been additions to it since its first definition, and 802.3 now covers a range of possibilities, from fast broadband systems using co-axial cable to 1 Mb/s twisted pair networks. What they have in common is that they are all linear networks - either a spine-and-arms bus or a daisy chain - and they use the CSMA/CD collision detection protocol.

Despite the variety, as long as the manufacturers have followed the specifications - particularly those that govern the interface between cable and computer - it should be possible to mix hardware and software from different sources in the one system. This may not be significant in the early days of a network, when it is always simplest to install a complete system, but it could become important later.

IEEE 802.4 - Token Bus Systems

This standard is based upon the 3M/Datapoint network, ARCnet, and is widely used in manufacturing environments. When computers are being used for process control regular, predictable access to the network is vital.

As we noted earlier, the collision-detection protocols of Ethernet systems result in random delays. As these are likely to be beyond human perception, they may not matter in a commercial office but when the networked computers are monitoring and controlling a production line, guaranteed feedback and response is essential.

IEEE 802.5 - Token Ring Systems

The 802.5 standard was written with the IBM token ring in mind and, at the time of writing, only covers the IBM system. As yet, few other manufacturers have shown much interest in this approach to networks but no doubt they will and, as they do, the 802.5 standard will expand to cover them.

As the token ring has been described above, there is no point in repeating it here.

Non-Technical Summary

The following is only relevant to PC networks in straightforward office environments. Where the network is to be used for process control or will be linked with mainframe computers or span out beyond the local area, then technical issues cannot be ignored. Sorry about that.

In most circumstances, the choice of network hardware and protocols is more or less irrelevant as all are equally capable of doing the job. A reliable and reputable supplier, who will still be around for years to maintain and extend your system, is worth far more than any degree of technical excellence.

If the network will never grow beyond half a dozen computers, then speed is not particularly important, because even a 1 Mb/s system will work fast enough for your human users. Where there may be up to 20 or 30 stations, you should look for a system that can run at 4 Mb/s, and faster for larger systems.

Twisted pair cable will usually be fine, but if there will be more than a few hundred metres between the two ends of the network - measuring as the cable lays, not as the crow flies - then use shielded twisted pair or co-axial cable (optic fibre if you are very hi-tech or wealthy).

Networking Standards

Though the cables and interfaces are the essential basis of any network, the useful work that you get out of it will depend greatly upon other factors. The speed and capacity of the file-server computers, the ease of use of the network-management software, the suitability of the applications programs and the quality of the training are all crucial to the functioning of the network. We shall look at all of these in later chapters.

5

Network Software

Cables and interface cards may create the physical net but it is the software that makes the net *work*. In this chapter we will look at what good software can do, and how it does it. The examples assume that the network consists of one hard disk computer, acting as file server, plus three floppy disk workstations. Printers are attached to the hard disk machine and one other. The examples are drawn from Sage's MainLan, but all good software works in much the same way.

Installation

When MainLan is installed in the computer with the hard disk, it creates a new directory, `\MAINLAN`, with three sub-directories.

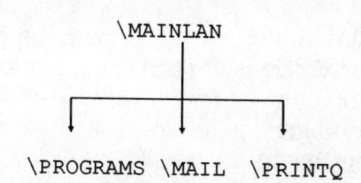

```
              \MAINLAN
        ┌────────┼────────┐
    \PROGRAMS  \MAIL   \PRINTQ
```

Network Software

`\PROGRAMS` stores the MainLan network software. The other two sub-directories are initially empty but will be used for the (temporary) storage of electronic mail and files for printing.

The installation process also creates a new `AUTOEXEC.BAT` file. This is the one that is run automatically by the computer's start-of-day routine. Before installation, a simple `AUTOEXEC.BAT` file would look like this:

```
echo off
set comspec=c:\msdos\command.com
keybuk
mouse
cls
```

The purpose of this file is to let the operating system know where it can find the core MS-DOS commands, set the keyboard to UK usages and install the mouse driver routines. Some files get more complicated as people add other instructions to configure their system the way they want it. For example, on a machine that was used mainly for word processing, it would be useful to write in commands to change to the relevant directory and get the word processor up and running. Other people might use the start-up file to run the `GRAPHICS.COM` utility, so that graphics can be printed by applications programs, or to load in a memory-resident utility.

The MainLan-adapted `AUTOEXEC.BAT` file will include this command which loads the major components of the network software into memory:

```
C:\MAINLAN\PROGRAMS\NET
```

With this done the computer will become an active part of the network as soon as it is turned on, without needing any special action from the user.

Installation on the floppy disk systems is a similar process. Here, it creates a new start of day disk containing the key MainLan software and an `AUTOEXEC.BAT` file which gets it up and running.

The rest of the installation routines are the same on all machines. You need to give the key specifications of each computer and provide unique names to identify each computer and printer on the network. These should be as simple and memorable as possible. On our example network, the central hard disk system might be named 'CENTRAL', and the others 'ACCOUNTS', 'STOCK' and 'TYPING'; the printers could be identified by type - 'DAISY' and 'DOT'.

Network Software

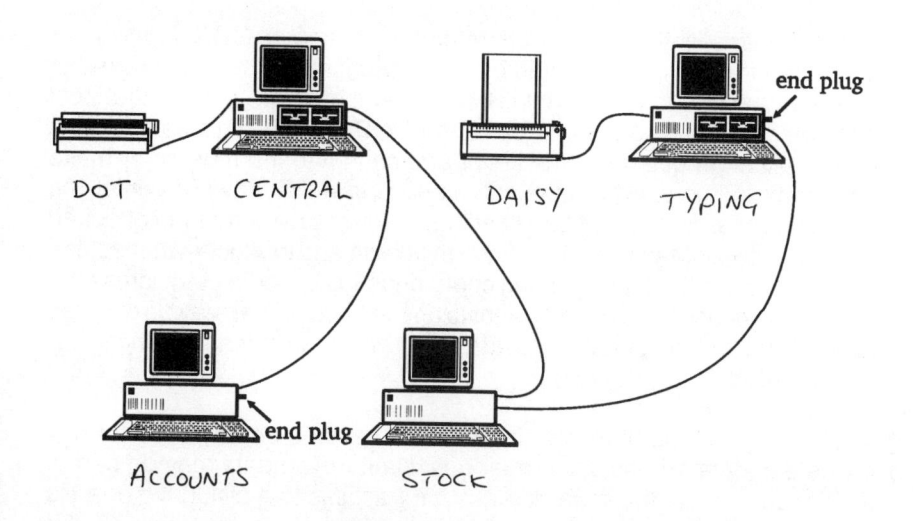

Figure 5.1 A 4-station network

In Use

The network software acts as a memory-resident utility. It sits in high memory, between the MS-DOS operating system and the area used by the applications programs. The full MainLan software takes a fair bit of space - anything up to 200K, depending upon the size of network and how it is used. This could create problems on 512K machines and with those applications that need a lot of memory but the full set is only needed on those stations which provide filing, mail and printing services to the rest. The software is divided into sections and it is possible to reduce the demands of the netware by removing those sections that are not needed at the time. A floppy disk workstation without a printer, for example, has no use for the programs which allow other users to share its disks and printer; that saves over 40K immediately. There are other utilities which can also be trimmed off without affecting the basic functions of the network - though there may be some loss of convenience.

The netware's functions can be divided into two main blocks: the NETBIOS, those low-level ones that run automatically, and the menu-driven commands that are performed on the direct instructions of a network user. The NETBIOS routines look both ways, inwards to activities of the individual computers and outwards to the network.

Network Software

The NETBIOS System

When an applications program attempts to use a DOS function or command the call is intercepted by the network software and checked to see if any action is necessary. Those calls that relate only to the local computer are passed straight on to the DOS system. This set includes those which get data from the keyboard, send it to the monitor or make use of the memory. Where the command is to a disk drive or printer the netware comes into play. If the drive that is being accessed is not attached to the computer, MainLan will redirect the command to whichever machine owns the drive. Similarly, printing commands will be redirected across the network if necessary; even files sent to an attached printer may be diverted to a queue for temporary storage if the printer is already working for another user.

The NETBIOS also monitors the network, keeping an ear open for any packets of data addressed to their host station. The data may be part of an electronic mail message, a request for access to a disk drive or a file sent for printing. At the head of each packet are a few bytes to identify the destination. Every station's netware will check that address and then either let the data go past or draw it off the network and deal with it as appropriate.

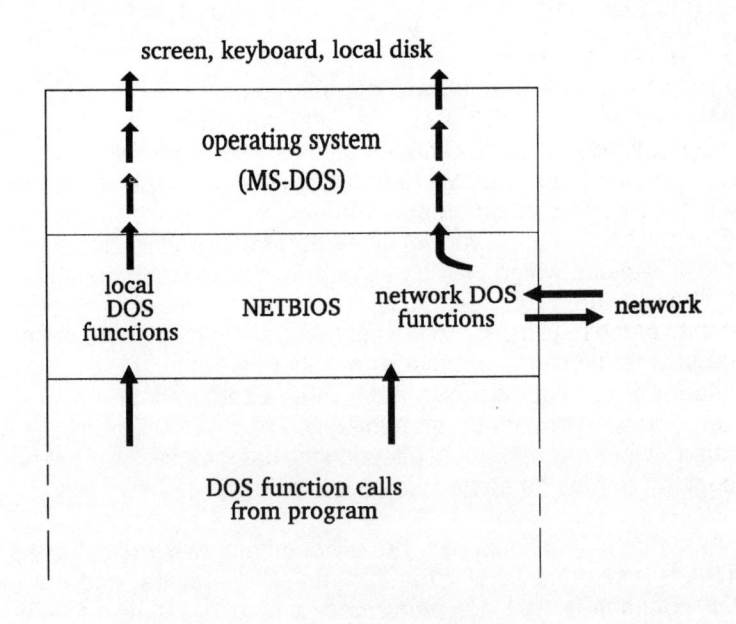

Figure 5.2 The NETBIOS routines in action

Network Software

The technical complexities of how the network software performs these functions can be safely left to the experts. For the working user, it is enough to know that they are there and that they can look after themselves.

The Network Commands

These high-level functions are all managed through a menu system. Under the normal set up, they are memory-resident and available via a 'Hot Key'; the combination of [Alt] and [Shift] calls them up from within whatever application program may be running at the time. If memory space is needed for a large program, then they can be left on disk and called up from the DOS prompt with the 'NET' command.

The MainLan commands are organised in a two-tier structure. Having called up the main menu, you select it by moving a highlight bar to the command set and pressing [Enter]. A sub-menu then appears and selection is made in the same way. With most commands you will then be presented with a fresh screen and a request for details. When the command has been performed, the system will return you to the second level menu. At any stage, a command can be aborted or a selection reversed by pressing [Esc]. Provided you have not removed the screen drivers from memory (which may have been necessary with a very greedy program), your previous screen will be restored. You will, in any case, be returned to whatever job you had been doing previously.

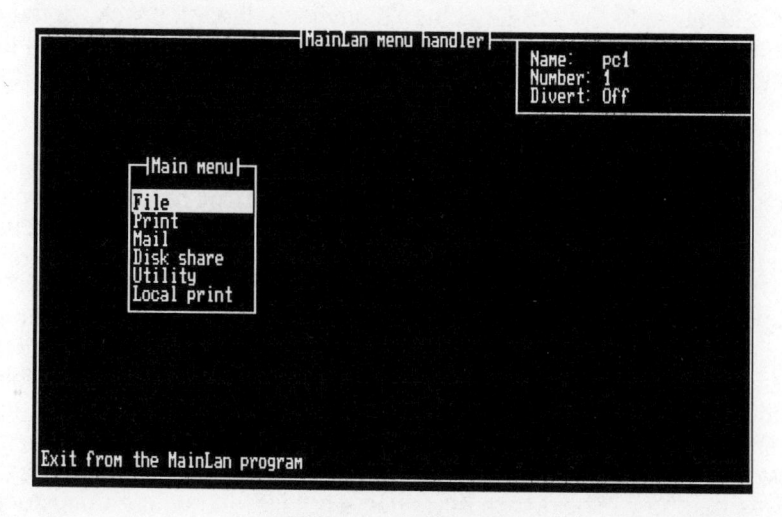

Figure 5.3 The Main Menu

Network Software

The File Set

MainLan gives you two means of accessing disk drives on other networked machines. Through the Disk Share commands it is possible to make a connection to a remote drive so that it acts as if it were attached to the user's computer. The File set are mainly intended for the simpler purpose of transferring occasional files across the network. They cannot be used to gain access to a drive or directory that has been password protected.

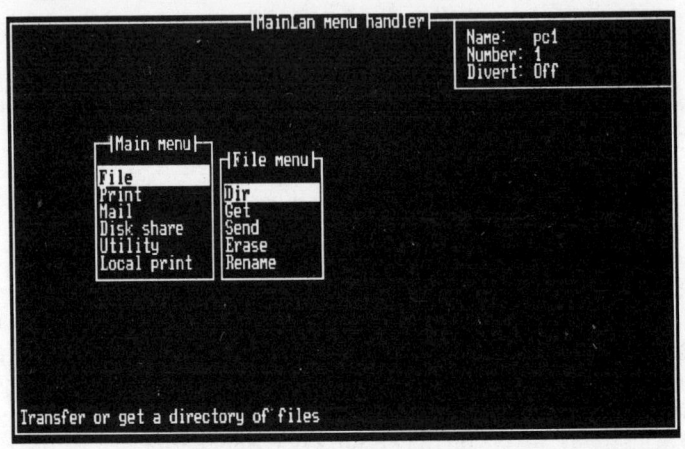

Figure 5.4 The File set

Dir is identical to the MS-DOS '`dir`' command, though it lacks some of the options. The details needed by this command are the name of the remote computer, its drive or directory and the file specification. This can include wildcards, just as in the normal DOS command.

Get and *Send* will copy individual or wildcard-selected files between a remote directory and the local disk drive. Note that files can only be copied onto a disk; they cannot be loaded into memory. For that, you must use the Disk Share commands.

Erase and *Rename* are the same as their MS-DOS equivalents, except that wildcards cannot be used in either. The minor inconvenience this may cause is as nothing compared to the problems that could arise by wiping whole sets of files in error! It should be a general rule on networks that users only erase or rename their own files. Password protection can be given to shared directories via the Disk Share commands and access to drives can be withheld from other users but files in common directories are vulnerable.

TIP. Protect your files with ATTRIB

The MS-DOS operating system does not allow you to set password protection on individual files; it was not needed on the single-user systems for which MS-DOS was designed. The only protection it affords is that files can be made Read Only, using the ATTRIB command.

```
C>ATTRIB +R letter.txt
```

This will prevent letter.txt from being altered or erased in error but if that file is in an open area, other users could remove the protection and then erase it. The erasure could be quite unintentional. A second person might have a set of .txt files there that he wished to edit but which had also been protected. To restore Read-Write permission - so that changes could be made - he would use this command:

```
C>ATTRIB -R *.txt
```

The file letter.txt will have been stripped of protection by the wildcard and could then be erased at any time. Security is always a potential problem on any network, and we shall return to it later.

The Disk Share Set

With these commands, more than any other, it is possible to see the network functioning as a single unit, rather than as a collection of linked machines. A network might be organised with all the word-processing software and data on one hard disk, spreadsheet materials on another, the accounts on a third and the business's database on a fourth, yet every user could run any program and treat part of each drive as if it were their own. Once the connections have been made through MainLan, the drives can be accessed by simple MS-DOS commands or from within programs.

Share is the key command in this set. It is the one which allows other people to connect up to your drive. It also enables passwords to be set so that only the hard disk owner and those who know the relevant passwords can gain access to the shared directories.

Normally you would only share space on a hard disk machine; there are few advantages and many hazards in sharing a floppy disk drive. If floppy-held files must be shared, copy them into a hard disk first or pass the actual disk across the office.

Network Software

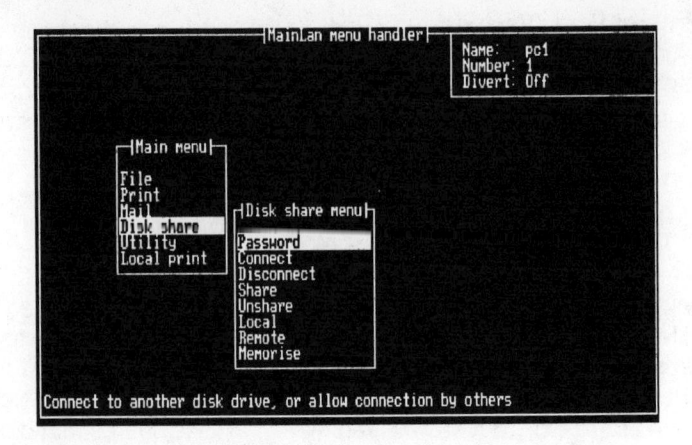

```
                    ─┤MainLan menu handler├─
                                            Name:    pc1
                                            Number:  1
                                            Divert:  Off

        ┌┤Main menu├─┐
        │ File       │
        │ Print      │
        │ Mail       │
        │ Disk share ├┤Disk share menu├─┐
        │ Utility    ││ Password        │
        │ Local print││ Connect         │
        └────────────┤│ Disconnect      │
                     ││ Share           │
                     ││ Unshare         │
                     ││ Local           │
                     ││ Remote          │
                     ││ Memorise        │
                     │└─────────────────┘

 Connect to another disk drive, or allow connection by others
```

Figure 5.5 The disk share set

Sharing is managed by the device of *named areas*. A drive or directory which is to be shared is given a name, quite independent of its official name. A little care is needed when setting up shared areas, for every sub-directory within an area is then open to sharing. You cannot have a private section within a shared area.

On our example network, the CENTRAL hard disk has a special directory for the word-processing software and common files, with separate sub-directories for each user's own private files. (Note that the actual structure of directories is nothing to do with the network software. It is purely a matter of how disks have been organised using the normal DOS commands. In practice, as we shall see later, you may need to reorganise your directories to make the best use out of them on the network.)

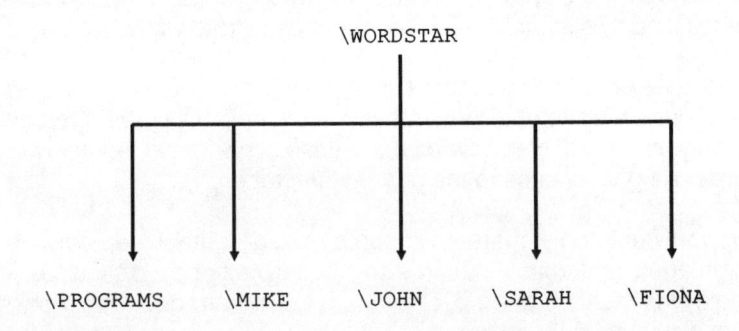

```
                         \WORDSTAR
              ┌─────┬───────┼───────┬──────┐
              ▼     ▼       ▼       ▼      ▼
          \PROGRAMS \MIKE  \JOHN  \SARAH  \FIONA
```

Figure 5.6 Example directory structure

Network Software

Using *Share* at the CENTRAL computer, the programs sub-directory, known to MS-DOS as C:\WORDSTAR\PROGRAMS, is named 'WORDS'. As this is to be open to all, no password is set. In the same way, the following areas are established.

Area	Name	Password
C:\WORDSTAR\MIKE	MIKEWS	Yes
C:\WORDSTAR\JOHN	JOHNWS	Yes
C:\WORDSTAR\SARAH	SARAHWS	Yes
C:\WORDSTAR\FIONA	FIONAWS	Yes

There is nothing to stop you using a directory name as an area name. John's sub-directory could have been identified by the existing name 'JOHN'. 'JOHNWS' was chosen as this will remind him that the area is within the WORDSTAR set.

Connect is used to gain access to a named area on a remote drive.

When John wants to use WordStar on another computer on the net he will call up the command and link the named area with a drive letter. The connected directory then acts as a 'virtual drive' of his own machine; MS-DOS treats it as if it were really attached to his computer. As John has a single-floppy machine, only the A: drive is present. Via Connect, he sets it so that the sub-directory known as 'WORDS' becomes virtual drive B:. Once that is done, he can escape from the MainLan menus and give the MS-DOS sequence:

```
A>B:      (switch to drive B:)
B>WS      (run WordStar)
```

In practice, he would normally want to connect to his WordStar files sub-directory before starting work but before he can do that he must first give the password.

Password must be used before *Connect* if the area is protected. The command appears at the top of the list to remind users of this. At first, it feels a little odd doing things this way round - most software will ask for the password after you have made the initial connection - but in practice it can work out to be quite convenient. If there are several areas that you may want to access, and all have the same password, it need only be given once, at the start of the session.

Network Software

Named Areas and Disk Use

Up to 16 areas can be named on the disk drives of any one computer. This should be enough for most purposes, though it may require some forethought in the organisation of disk space. In the example above, four areas had been taken for the word processing alone. This doesn't leave many for other activities, and some compromises had to be made to fit them all in. As you can see from the structure shown here, named areas were only allocated to those people who particularly needed private file storage. Other users have to keep their files either on their own floppy disks - and not make use of the networked drive - or place them along with the common files in the main \PROGRAM sub-directory in each set. The ACCOUNTS files are not divided as they are the common property of the whole office.

Directory structure

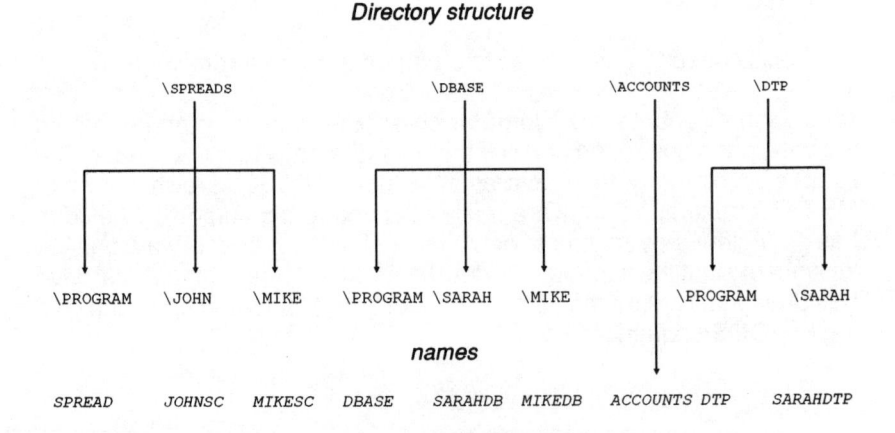

```
        \SPREADS                    \DBASE              \ACCOUNTS      \DTP
       /    |    \                 /    |    \              |            |
\PROGRAM  \JOHN  \MIKE       \PROGRAM \SARAH \MIKE     \PROGRAM      \SARAH
```

names

SPREAD   JOHNSC   MIKESC   DBASE   SARAHDB   MIKEDB   ACCOUNTS DTP   SARAHDTP

Figure 5.7 Named areas

This was by no means the only, and was certainly not the most efficient, way that our firm could have divided the disks into areas. It was one that grew out of the existing structure of sub-directories on the hard disk, and has been accepted because it is simple to use. If Sarah knows that she will use the word-processing, database and desktop publishing programs during a working session, she can make connections to them all at the start. It will then be as if she had six additional disk drives attached to her machine, with each one being used for a different purpose. If data needs to transferred from one area to another it can be done as simply as from A: to B: on a normal double-drive computer.

Network Software

Area	Drive letter
WORDS	C:
SARAHWS	D:
DBASE	E:
SARAHDB	F:
DTP	G:
SARAHDTP	H:

The choice of drive letters is purely arbitrary, and quite independent of what any other network user is doing. One area can be linked simultaneously to different drive letters on other computers; and several people may use the same drive letter to connect to different areas. It doesn't matter. Those letters only have meaning within the *redirectors* - the stations that are redirecting their data to remote disk drives. It is the area names which are fixed throughout the network.

We will return to the organisation of shared disks in the next chapter. Meanwhile, let's wrap up the rest of this set of commands.

Disconnect is used at the redirector to end the link to a named area; and *Unshare* closes off access to a shared area by removing its name. This command can only be given at the file server (the one which owns the shared drive), and for obvious reasons should only be used by the network manager or with the consent of other users.

Remote produces a list of the remote directories connected to the local computer, along with their drive letters.

Memorise records the named areas on a shared disk, or the links made by a connecting station. This command must be used at the file server if areas are to be permanently available. At the other end of the line, memorising links will mean that when the redirector is started up another day connections will be made automatically. This can be a useful time-saver, though links to password-protected areas should not be memorised in the interests of security. Otherwise, anyone with access to the start-up disk - or who can turn on a hard-disk system - will also have access to those confidential files. On our example network, most users have opted to memorise only the links to the common file and programs areas and make fresh connections to their private areas as needed. Mike's solution to the security problem is to memorise all his connections on the start-up disk but keep this under lock and key.

Network Software

The Printer Set

In practical terms, sharing a printer is often more difficult than sharing a disk drive. There are a number of reasons for this. Partly it is a question of speed; a file can be transferred to a disk drive far quicker than it can be printed, so that even under intensive use, disk-filing causes few delays. Access is another factor; each printer can only handle one file at a time. Other problems arise from the nature of MS-DOS, for that system was designed on the assumption that the user might have several drives but only a single printer; and human intervention cannot be ignored - a rushed or careless user can very easily leave a printer off-line, misaligned or out of paper.

When a computer is first brought into the network the installation routine will ask whether or not it has a printer attached. If it has, MainLan assumes that output is to be sent there; if not, the user will be asked for the name of the printer that will normally be used. Printers attached to networked computers do not have to be shared. They may be reserved for local use either permanently or temporarily; the Local Print set handles this. And the choice of printer is not final, as output may be diverted to any other shared printer at any time.

It is worth stressing that these - as all other MainLan commands - can be called up from within an applications program. So, when word processing, you might run off a quick draft on the dot matrix printer to check layout before getting a final daisywheel copy. The switch from one to the other could be done without breaking off from the word processor.

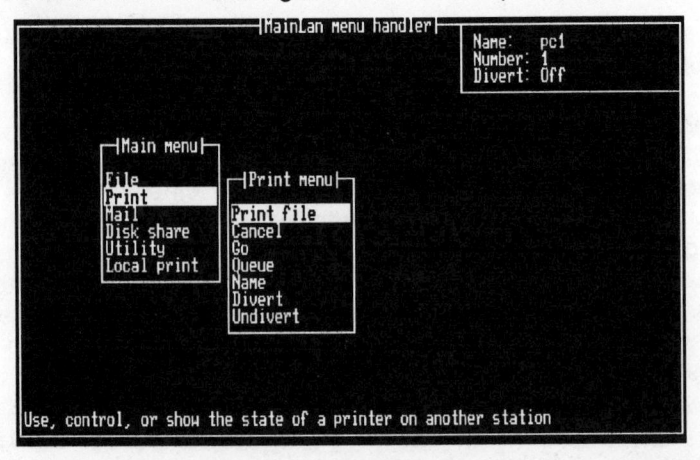

Figure 5.8 The Printer set

Network Software

Print File is used where the output from an applications program has been sent to a file, rather than direct to a printer. This might be done either because the paper copy is not wanted at the time or because the chosen printer is unavailable. Print File is also handy for one-off jobs - for the person who usually runs off the accounts summaries on the dot matrix but needs the crisp finish of a daisywheel for a special report. In our sample office, both printers tend to be under greatest pressure during the later part of the afternoon as people try to catch the last post. To ease the load, they have agreed to output non-urgent printing as files and then run these off the following morning with the Print File command.

The *Name* command is used to specify the printer to which output will be diverted, and must be used before Divert.

Queue gives a list of the files waiting to printed on the currently selected printer. Where a file needs to be printed in a hurry this command, in conjunction with Name, will let you check round the available printers to see which is least busy.

Cancel will remove one of your own files from a print queue; you may have found a quicker place to print it while waiting for it to work its way through a queue.

Go forces the immediate printing of a file - queues permitting - over-riding the normal short delay.

Divert redirects output from the normal printer to the one which has been selected by Name. This diversion lasts until cancelled by *Undivert*.

Mike, who handles most of the accounting, has his PC set up so that his files normally go to the dot matrix printer, DOT. When he wants to send out debt-chasing letters, he uses Name and Divert to switch output to DAISY. He then runs the debt routine in his accountancy package and switches back to DOT at the end with Undivert.

The Local Print Set

These give control of a printer and its print queue but may only be used at the PC to which it is attached. As they can interfere with the work of others, the commands should be used sparingly and with the knowledge of those who may be affected.

Network Software

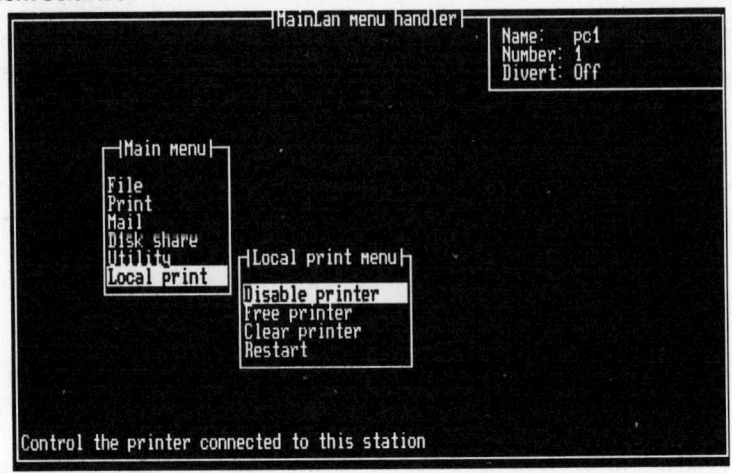

Figure 5.9 The Local Print set

Disable removes a printer from the network, so that it may only be used by the local computer. Any job currently in progress will be completed but those in the queue will have to wait until network printing is restored by *Free*.

Clear is an emergency command, designed to be used in the event of printer failure. It stops whatever job is being printed and removes any that may be in the queue.

The *Restart* command would be given if a printer had run out of paper or become jammed in the middle of a job. This will restart the job from the beginning.

The Mail Set

The usefulness of these commands depends to a large extent on the physical layout of the network. A small network, existing within a single office, will have all its users within sight and earshot of each other. In such circumstances, there will only be a few situations in which it makes sense to send messages across the network. But where users are separated by walls or by distance then these are handy, for the Mail does get through!

When mail is sent, a message will appear across the top of the screen at the destination, informing the recipient that a new message has arrived. The rest of the message will be stored - normally on the hard disk of the central PC.

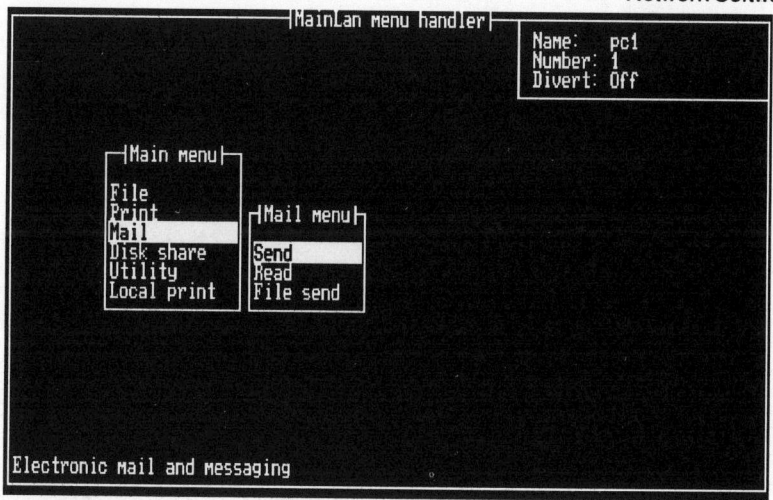

Figure 5.10 The Mail set

You can *Send* mail to a single station, everyone on the network or a selected list of stations. The routine has a simple but efficient text editor that is quite adequate for creating short memos. There is no limitation on the length of messages but, in practice, if you wanted to send a long document it would be easier to produce it with a word processor, then use the File Send command.

Read displays a list of the mail in your 'in-tray', each identified by a short title and its time and place of origin. Any item can be selected from the list and processed in one of four ways. An *Answer* will return the message to sender, with your comments appended; *Forward* will pass it on to someone else, always the easiest way to deal with tricky items; *Store* transfers it to an ordinary text file, which can then be loaded into a word processor; and *Delete* removes it from the list.

File Send is similar to Send, in that you start by giving the destination(s) and a title, but instead of using the Mail text editor, you send a prepared text file. In our sample office the secretary makes use of this to send draft letters to people when they must be checked before committing them to paper.

The Utility Set

These are mainly concerned with the state of the network, and apart from 'Who' will probably receive only occasional use.

Network Software

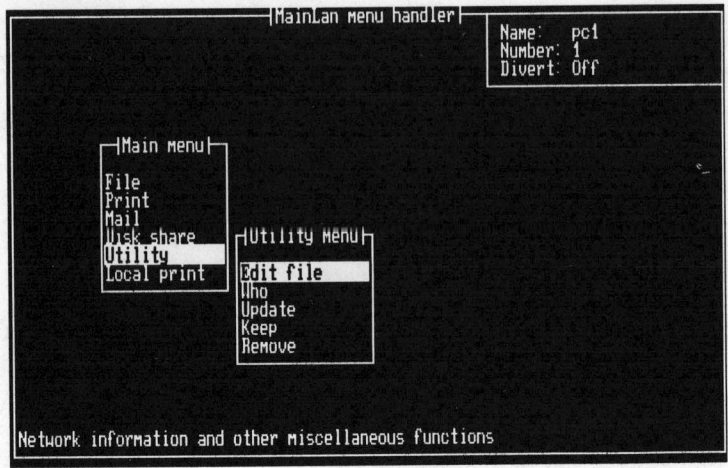

```
┤MainLan menu handler├
                       Name:   pc1
                       Number: 1
                       Divert: Off

       ┤Main menu├
       File
       Print
       Mail
       Disk share  ┤Utility menu├
       Utility     Edit file
       Local print Who
                   Update
                   Keep
                   Remove


Network information and other miscellaneous functions
```

Figure 5.11 The Utility set

Edit File gives access to the same text editor that is used by the Mail. It can be handy for jotting down notes while in the middle of an applications program.

Who produces a list of the stations, and printers, currently on the network. At its most basic level it provides a check on the functioning of the network itself but it is also very handy for finding out who is around to receive mail, and which printers are available for use.

Update saves to disk any alterations to the names of computers, printers and shared directories.

Sometimes, as a means of saving memory space, you may choose not to load the MainLan menus into memory but to take them from disk, as and when needed. If this has been done, *Keep* will store the menu routines once memory becomes available; while *Remove* will take them out, releasing more space.

Summary

The facilities offered by network software fall into three groups, relating to disk sharing, printer sharing and electronic mail.

Shared access to disks will allow people to share programs and data files. Data may also be shared by transferring files either by mail, or by the disk-filing commands.

File and print servers have more control over their attached peripherals than do the other workstations. The users of servers must therefore take a greater share of the responsibility for their peripherals.

Planning a Networked System

6

Analysing Your Requirements

It's very tempting to just let a network grow, without ever bothering to sit down and plan it, especially if you are starting small. After all, a network may consist of no more than two PC's sharing a printer and a hard disk. Does that need planning? I would say, 'yes it does', because that 2-station net is very likely to grow over time and, if you are not careful, you will run up against limits that could have been foreseen.

A network does not exist in isolation from the rest of the office; it is very much a part of it. If it is to function successfully it must reflect the organisation of the office and be tailored to fit its information needs. Any attempt to plan a network must therefore start, not with hardware or networking packages, but with a close look at the office itself. You need to define the existing situation, the problems for which you seek solutions and the improvements that you would like. It takes a little time but it can save an awful lot of bother.

Analysing Your Requirements

The current use of computers is crucial. To what extent and for what purposes does the business already use computers? Does this form a sound foundation upon which a network could be built or is it time for a complete rethink? Fortunately, networks are much more flexible and forgiving than those multi-user systems built around mainframes or mini-computers. A network can be created in stages, evolving from the existing computing base and being extended steadily as money allows and information needs dictate - though the main lines of development must be clear from the start. By contrast, installing a multi-user system will generally mean making an almost complete break from the past, with new hardware, new software and a major change in office procedures. It follows from this that if a multi-user installation is not planned properly, alteration and upgrading will be difficult and expensive.

People must be considered carefully. What tasks and responsibilities do they undertake at present, and what may they take on in future? The introduction of a network will inevitably change the work of the office to some extent and much of this can be foreseen and prepared for. What level of computing skills do the staff have, and what may they reasonably be expected to acquire? A powerful but complex system could be a boon in a hi-tech office with computer-literate staff but a disaster if key personnel were unwilling or unable to learn the skills needed to run it.

The physical layout of the office will obviously have implications for the actual installation of the network, and the question of where to locate file and print servers needs to be borne in mind from the outset. And 'where to locate' really means 'whose desk?', for that will largely determine who is responsible for backing up the hard disk or for ensuring that printers are kept running smoothly.

Most of all, data is the key. What quantity and type of data is in circulation within the office; what comes in for processing; what outputs are required; how much needs to be stored? In all of these questions, 'data' is used in the general sense of information in any form; it may be customers' accounts, invoices, suppliers' details, stock lists, personnel files, memos, minutes of meetings; it may be on computer disk, on paper or transferred by word of mouth. It is all data, and some or all of it may be better handled across a network.

The assumptions underlying the rest of this chapter are that yours is a business which is already using one or more computers for some tasks, and that you are fairly clear about any additional software that you would like to use in the foreseeable future. There will always be applications not yet considered - perhaps not yet produced - that may well become important in years to come. Their arrival can be anticipated by leaving some slack in your system and by making sure that there is a clear upgrade path open to you.

Applications Programs

The best place to start your plan is with the applications programs that you are or will be running. Some of these will be existing single-user software, others multi-user - either versions of programs already in use or bought specially for the new network. For each of these, you should perform a breakdown of its needs in terms of processing power, disk storage and peripheral usage. A standard form will help to get the information together (Figure 6.1).

Workstation

How much RAM memory is needed by the program? Older programs, and some of the smaller new ones, can run happily in 512K or even 256K but many of today's all-singing, all-dancing products are designed for 640K computers. The nominal RAM requirement is a useful guide but it is not enough. You need to know how much space is actively used, for the network software will be taking up memory in every workstation.

As a general rule, multi-user software will be more economical in its use of space than its single-user equivalent because network-ability would have been part of its design; and a 640K PC should be able to cope with any 512K program without trouble. (SageSoft have yet to find a multi-user product that will not work on a 640K PC running under MainLan, and they have tried software from such market leaders as Lotus, MicroSoft, Computer Associates and Borland.)

The type of processor will be irrelevant for most business software but specialist products, CAD for example, may need a high performance 80286 or 80386 processor: the sort found in PC AT's. Likewise, the choice of monitor - monochrome, CGA, EGA or VGA colour - may be a matter of personal preference with most applications but high resolution would be needed wherever graphics played a major role.

If every computer user in the office is to have their own PC then the percent usage figures can be omitted. These are only needed if machines are to be shared. Note that even occasional users should have their own PC if sharing would cause expensive or inconvenient delays.

Analysing Your Requirements

Disk Storage

In normal use, data storage will be divided between hard disks and floppies but what goes where depends upon the type of file and upon who needs access to it. When working out storage requirements you must look at each user's need for each application. Some networks will require more than one hard disk; it will depend upon the total quantity of data and whothor or not particular programs will work best with access to a local drive. Though floppy disk storage must be considered, it is only shared and local hard disk capacity that is relevant for planning.

Program files will generally all go onto a hard disk, partly for speed and convenience of loading, partly so that all users may have the use of it at any time. (Some programs will only work if their overlay files are on hard disk.) Floppy disk storage may be worth considering for programs that are used rarely and by few individuals.

Any data files that are to be shared must be on hard disk. You can never guarantee that a floppy will be in the right place at the right time.

By *private* files, I mean those in which other network users will not or should not have any interest. Those that are truly confidential are probably best kept on floppy disks, for at least these can be locked away when not in use. Others may be stored either on a local or a remote (shared) hard disk. Write in a figure for local storage only if speed of access is important, or with those single-user programs that will not work across the net.

With any hard disk, regular housekeeping is needed to prevent this from clogging up with old files. It's remarkably easy to fill up megabytes of disk space with copies of old correspondence, spreadsheets once used and long forgotten and sorted database files that were only on disk as a prelude to printing. One solution is to allocate a reasonable amount of working storage for each user on each application and ask them to keep within this. Files that are no longer needed on a regular basis can be transferred to floppy for permanent storage.

Printer Access

How much access time does each user need for each type of printer? In Figure 6.1 the types are Draft and Quality but in some circumstances a dot matrix printer with a Near Letter Quality facility will be enough; in others you may need dot matrix, daisywheel and laser.

Analysing Your Requirements

The percentage usage should be an estimated average, erring on the side of generosity and remembering that a printer may be unavailable to other users even though it is not actually printing. The one at the sales counter that prints the invoices will be loaded with invoice blanks and can be used for nothing else while the door is open to customers; the receptionist/ secretary may need to have complete control of her daisywheel.

It is worth noting that the existence of the network may reduce the overall amount of printing. If people can access data via their PC's they may not need printed copies of price lists, stock lists, contacts, addresses and the like. The effective use of electronic mail can cut down the number of memos and draft copies of letters.

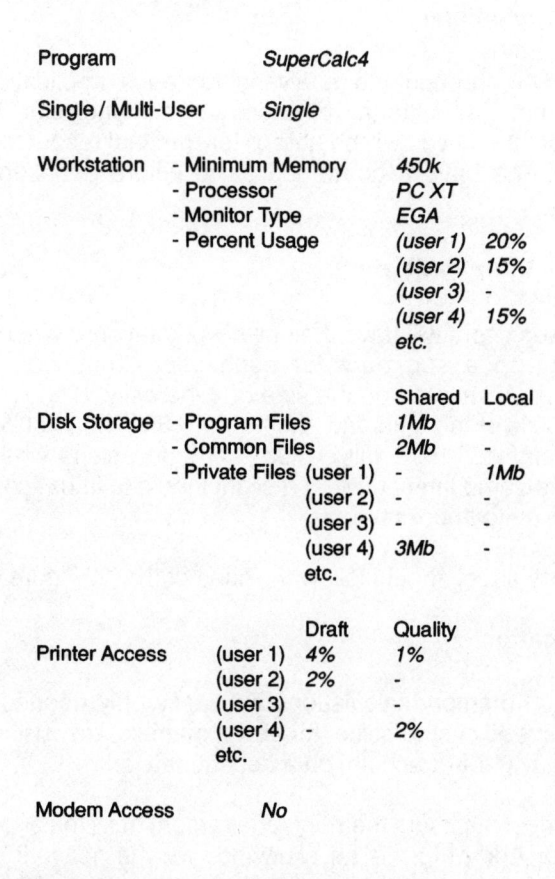

Program		*SuperCalc4*	
Single / Multi-User		*Single*	
Workstation	- Minimum Memory	*450k*	
	- Processor	*PC XT*	
	- Monitor Type	*EGA*	
	- Percent Usage	(user 1) *20%*	
		(user 2) *15%*	
		(user 3) -	
		(user 4) *15%*	
		etc.	
		Shared	Local
Disk Storage	- Program Files	*1Mb*	-
	- Common Files	*2Mb*	-
	- Private Files (user 1)	-	*1Mb*
	(user 2)	-	-
	(user 3)	-	-
	(user 4)	*3Mb*	-
	etc.		
		Draft	Quality
Printer Access	(user 1)	*4%*	*1%*
	(user 2)	*2%*	-
	(user 3)	-	-
	(user 4)	-	*2%*
	etc.		
Modem Access		*No*	

Figure 6.1 Application program analysis

Modem Access

This is the most difficult peripheral to share, for it can only ever be used by one person at a time. There are also substantial technical difficulties in using a modem across a network and the facility is only found in the more sophisticated and expensive network software. You could attach a modem to a computer on a MainLan network, but only where it would not come into conflict with the network functions - which means not on a machine that acted as a server. Modems are not expensive and the simplest solution is often to fit one to each PC that is used for external communications. Make a note of each program that may need one.

Drawing Conclusions

Having worked through the analyses for each application, you can produce summaries in terms of users/workstations, data storage and printers. From these you will be able to tell the total resources needed by the network and have a good idea as to where peripherals are best located.

Users and Workstations

In many cases users will have their own workstations. Where they are to share, draw up a summary for each user, then look for suitable combinations. Always err on the side of generosity. If one person needs access for 60% of the time and another for 25%, the total is too close to 100% for comfort. There will be too many occasions when both want access at the same time and only a slight increase in usage would make the situation quite impossible.

The summary sheet should follow the lines of that in Figure 6.2.

PC Specification

The minimum memory calculations are really only needed if you have 512K PC's already in the office, for all the mainstream business software will run on any 640K machine, on a decent network.

Find the highest minimum memory requirement of all the applications that will be used. Add onto this an allowance for the network software (for MainLan, this will be a minimum of 50K, rising to 150K+ if the workstation has a shared disk and printer and is used for central mail storage.) Few memory-resident programs work well on a network but if one is essential,

Analysing Your Requirements

then add in its memory requirement. From the total, you should be able to see whether or not a 512K PC will be adequate. If not, existing 512K machines can be easily upgraded to 640K if they have a spare expansion slot for the additional memory card.

Where a high-performance processor or a very high resolution monitor is demanded by an application program it may be worth looking carefully at the amount the program is used. If it has only occasional usage by several people, could they share a single high-specification machine for this work? Access to a *modem* should be looked at in the same light.

Local Hard Disk Storage

If the local hard disk storage figure is very small - no more than a few megabytes - then see if a shared remote disk could possibly be used. If

```
PC Specification
    Memory      640k
    Processor   -
    Monitor Type  EGA

    Percent Usage   (app. 1)    10%
                    (app. 2)    5%
                    (app. 3)    20%
                    (app. 4)    15%
                    Total       50%

    Local Hard Disk Storage
                    (app. 1)    2Mb
                    (app. 2)    -
                    (app. 3)    5Mb
                    (app. 4)    -
                    Total       7Mb

                                Draft   Quality
    Printer Access  (app. 1)    5%      -
                    (app. 2)    -       5%
                    (app. 3)    10%     -
                    (app. 4)    5%      2%
                    Total       20%     7%

    Modem Access    No
```

Figure 6.2 User/workstation summary

Analysing Your Requirements

a local disk is essential, there is no point at this stage of trying to specify the size; that will depend upon the overall data storage requirements.

Printer Access

Each PC's printer access should be noted, as the logical arrangement would be to attach printers to those PC's that make most use of them. Totals for the whole office will determine the actual number of printers. You should tackle printers next, before data storage, for if a print server is to handle its queues efficiently it must have a hard disk.

Printers and Print Servers

Start by working out the total usage of each type of printer and from that calculate the number of each that will be needed. No machine should ever be 100% in use. If the usage is anywhere near that figure there will be unacceptable delays at times when over-long queues build up, and there will be little slack in the system to cope with mechanical failure or paper and ink problems. In the example in Figure 6.3, the Draft printer is expected to run at 60% capacity. This should be acceptable but at 75% or more there could be trouble.

There are several possible solutions. One is to direct more of the printing to an under-used machine but the effectiveness of this will depend upon the type of printer. In the example, the Quality printer has surplus capacity but, as this will be significantly slower than the Draft one, redirecting even 5% of output to it could increase its loading by 20% or 30%. If a daisywheel printer were under pressure but there was spare time on a dot matrix, redirection would probably not be possible, simply because of the poor quality of the output.

Printer Access

	Draft	Quality
User 1	*20%*	*7%*
User 2	*15%*	*3%*
User 3	*10%*	*15%*
User 4	*15%*	*8%*
Totals	*60%*	*33%*

Figure 6.3 Printer access

Analysing Your Requirements

If a more efficient use of existing printers is not possible, then either add new ones or replace the over-used ones with faster models. A machine running at 160 characters per second has twice the capacity of one at 80 c.p.s. Both approaches mean buying new equipment but, if a new printer is added, you may also need another hard disk to cope with its print queue.

Every printer that is to be used across the network must have a print server - its controlling computer. This server must be able to cope with the demands of the print queue, which doesn't just mean that it needs a hard disk. Servicing the queue will take processing time and disk time and if the server is also somebody's workstation - which is often the case - then it must be powerful enough to meet the needs of its user and of the network. We will return to the subject of servers, along with other types of hardware, in the next chapter.

Data Storage Requirements

For this you will need a summary sheet showing the disk space needed for program files, common data files and individual users' private files, both remote and local. From this you should be able to see which PC's must have a hard disk and how much capacity is needed in total.

App. Name	Program	Common	User 1	User 2	User 3	User 4
Accounts	1Mb	8Mb	-	-	-	-
WordStar	1Mb	3Mb	2Mb	-	4Mb	2Mb
SuperCalc	1Mb	2Mb	1Mb	3Mb	-	1Mb
dBase	2Mb	12Mb	-	2Mb	-	-
Finesse	1Mb	-	1Mb	-	5Mb	-
Local	-	-	-	3Mb	4Mb	-
TOTALS	6Mb	25Mb	4Mb	8Mb	13Mb	3Mb	59Mb

Figure 6.4 Data storage requirements

In our example in Figure 6.4, the workstations of users 2 and 3 should have hard disks and - at the moment - 59 Megabytes are required. This figure should be doubled to allow room for expansion. From the previous summary, we can see that the Quality printer will be best attached to workstation 3 but usage of the Draft model is spread fairly evenly. User 1

Analysing Your Requirements

has the highest percentage but not by that great a margin. This printer could be located either there - which would then need a hard disk - or at workstation 2. For the sake of argument we will assume that in this example other considerations of office organisation - physical layout and job responsibilities - dictate that the Draft printer must be attached to workstation 1.

Workstation 1		Workstation 2		Workstation 3	
User 1	4Mb	User 2	8Mb	User 3	13Mb
Programs	6Mb				
Common	25Mb				
User	3Mb				
Total	38Mb		8Mb		13Mb
Size	65Mb		20Mb		20Mb

Figure 6.5 Data storage allocation: option 1

In this situation, where there will be three hard disks, there are two approaches to the allocation of data storage. One is to concentrate as much as possible, so that one PC becomes the file server for the network and the other two act only as print servers, with local hard disk storage. In the example, this could be managed with a 65 Megabyte drive on workstation 1 and 20 Megabyte drives on 2 and 3. At these sizes, all the hard disks have room for print queues and for later expansion (Figure 6.5).

Workstation 1		Workstation 2		Workstation 3	
User 1	4Mb	User 2	8Mb	User 3	13Mb
Programs			6Mb		
Common	15Mb		5Mb		5Mb
User 4					3Mb
Total	19Mb		19Mb		21Mb
Size	40Mb		40Mb		40Mb

Figure 6.6 Data storage allocation: option 2

Such a concentration can make backing up easier and will reduce the network's demands on the other two PC's. Conversely, it does put a heavy load on the machine designated as the file server. How well this is able to cope will depend upon the type of PC that it is and the amount of local use that it gets.

Analysing Your Requirements

The alternative approach is to spread the storage around the system; even the common files can be stored on several drives, as long as related ones are kept together. Spreading the file-server functions does put an extra load on several machines but it may prevent one from being overloaded; and if files are kept at the workstation where they are most used, then they can be accessed more quickly. The major disadvantage with this system is that the responsibility of backing up common files will be split between several users and there is a greater likelihood that the job will not be done properly, especially when people are off sick or on holiday.

At the end of this planning exercise you should be able to see how many PC's, printers and hard disks are needed and have some idea of the size and level of performance required from each. The next stage is to convert this outline plan into detailed specifications.

7

Hardware for the Network

The chances are that any firm that is contemplating setting up a network will already have a number of PC's and would prefer to spend as little as possible on new machines. The key questions are therefore 'Are the existing PC's up to the job?' and, if not, 'What extra equipment do we need?'

Let's start at the bottom. If you still have any of the early 256K or 320K machines about the place, it's time to trade them in. In theory, you could use them on some types of network - Torus Tapestry, for example, specifies 320K as the minimum for a workstation - but in practice they are unlikely to have enough memory to be able to spare some for the network software. Indeed, at that size they cannot even manage most modern applications programs when working as stand-alone PC's.

Your planning exercise should have revealed whether or not any 512K computers would be usable as they stand. There could well be people

Hardware for the Network

who only use smaller programs. If not, expansion cards (to upgrade them to 640K) are cheap and easy to install, though this may not always be possible. An Amstrad 1512, for example, has only three expansion slots. One of these must be used for the network adaptor. Put a RAM card in the second and there is only one left. If you had hoped to fit a hard disk *and* a modem onto that computer, you would be disappointed.

A 640K PC will certainly be usable as a workstation on the network and will have sufficient memory to function as a server. The question here is whether or not it has a sufficiently powerful processor to work either as a dedicated server or as a combined server and workstation. It may well have but it depends on how much of a workload is put on by its user and by the network.

The original IBM PC, and some current PC clones, use the Intel 8088 processor, a 16-bit chip with an 8-bit bus. Never mind the technicalities, what that means is that it moves data round in 8-bit chunks but it can cope with 16-bit numbers (anything up to 65535) when it is doing sums with them or using them to address memory. If it has heavy number-crunching to do, or is managing more than 64K of memory, it has to work a little harder. Better PC's have an Intel 8086 processor - a true 16-bit chip - and run it faster, so that the overall performance is considerably enhanced. The PC is a good workhorse but it has its limitations. It cannot handle more than 640K of memory, without special hardware and software, and it can run only one program at a time; when you call up the network functions or use any other memory-resident software, the current process is suspended.

The second generation of PC's are the IBM AT and its clones, all based around the Intel 80286 range of processors. These are 32-bit chips, though with a 16-bit bus - an echo of the 8088. Faster by design, they can also be run at a higher speed than the earlier chips (though it is worth noting that some new high-speed 8086 PC's can outperform older, slower PC AT's). They are capable of multi-tasking, given the right operating system, are generally supplied with 1 Megabyte of RAM memory and can manage up to 16 Megabytes if required. The 80286 is also used as the basis for the IBM PS/2 series of machines and its OS/2 operating system. At the time of writing, OS/2 was still suffering from substantial teething problems but it may become significant in future. Any 80286-based machine should be capable of running OS/2, with only minor adaptations.

At the top of today's market are those PC's with Intel 80386 processors. These are full 32-bit chips, with multi-tasking and multi-user capabilities. They have the power to cope with very demanding CAD or other graphics applications, while in another mode of operation a single 80386 can behave as if it were several independent 8086 chips. Such a machine can therefore act as the central processor in a multi-user system, run a number of programs on screen simultaneously or - more importantly in this context - manage network functions while it continues to work for the person at its keyboard.

Dedicated File Servers

Until recently, most network designs demanded the presence of a dedicated file server - a computer whose main purpose was to manage the hard disk and to service other stations' requests for data. It might also run a printer and have some network-management functions but it would not be available for use as a workstation. This was a reasonable arrangement when hard disks were expensive and their servers were running on relatively slow processors.

Today's new networks reflect the realities of today's PC's. Powerful processors and hard disks are cheap. The top of the range Amstrad 2386, with a fast, 32-bit processor, 65 Megabyte drive and high-resolution colour monitor comes in at around £3000 - in real terms no more than the 64K IBM PC, when it first appeared. And you can pick up an AT clone with a 40 Mb drive for under £1000. The trend over the next few years must be towards greater use of these more powerful machines and for many purposes they are considerably more powerful than is necessary.

Few people ever can or need to drive them flat out. When word processing, doing routine accounts chores, running small spreadsheets or similar jobs, the user would scarcely notice the difference between a PC XT or a new 386-based machine. The spreadsheet may be recalculated a few fractions of a second faster, a block may be moved from one end of a document to the other in the twinkling of an eye rather than in two twinkles but data entry always progresses at human speeds, and data entry is what takes up most of the time on most applications. In these circumstances, it makes sense to use some of the processor's surplus capacity by sharing it across a network.

A PC with an 80386 processor and a fast hard disk is capable of acting as a file server to a dozen other users while it continues to function as an ordinary workstation. One based on the 80286 processor - that is, the standard PC AT - should be able to service six users across the network and one at the keyboard. Even today's common or garden PC, with its humble 8086 processor, can afford to spend part of its time sharing its

Hardware for the Network

disk without affecting its normal performance too much. It is for this reason that the new networks, such as MainLan, are designed to allow any number of PC's to share their disks, rather than having a single dedicated file server.

The Sharing Workstation

You may have noticed that I keep dodging the question of under what circumstances an ordinary PC can be happily used as a workstation and file server. So, let's try to get down to some specifics.

For a start, there is a very simple answer if you have got the PC's there already. Try it. Set up the network and see what happens. If your file-serving workstation is struggling under the load, then you are going to have to buy a new and better machine. On the other hand, if you know that you are going to have to buy at least one more PC for the new network, and would prefer to spend as little as possible, then read on and try to assess what level of performance will be needed.

As a general rule, if there are less than half a dozen stations on the network, a standard PC should be able to share its hard disk without noticeably compromising its own performance. This is particularly the case if, as a workstation, it is mainly used for activities such as word processing, which do not make much use of the disk themselves. Some delays might be noticed if it were being used for accounting or for database work, where files are being regularly accessed. The other side of the equation is the level of demand being placed upon the server by the other stations. It is possible to get very technical about this and perform intensive analyses of disk use but this is rarely worth the effort. At the end of the day, the question is whether to buy a £1400 PC, a £1700 PC AT or a £3000 386 machine; from bottom to top, the difference wouldn't pay for the cost of such a work study. You can get a reasonable idea of the level of disk use by looking at and listening to the existing PC's while they work as stand-alone machines. If their disks are silent for long periods at a time, then they are not going to generate much demand on the network, and the one which is used least is the best machine to act as the file server.

If it looks as though an ordinary PC may have to struggle to meet the dual demands of the network and its user, then there are several options open. One is to use that PC only as a file server and buy another to take over its workstation role. A second is to split the disk-sharing with a second station, though this may have little effect in a network that revolves around a single activity. If most people spend most of their time processing the accounts, then the second server will do little to lift the load. The third option is to get a high-performance PC to handle the file serving or upgrade the existing machine by giving it a better processor.

Between six and twelve machines, you would almost certainly need to have a 286 or, better still, a 386-based PC in the network. Quite apart from giving greatly improved file-service, you will appreciate its speed for the electronic mail, which must have a central server.

On larger networks, you could split the disk-sharing over a number of 386 PC's or treat one as a dedicated file-server, perhaps pressing it into use occasionally. Here, as in the smaller PC networks, a lot depends upon the amount of disk-accessing and the nature of the activities at the workstations. In all networks, the server/workstation will continue to function even if it is over-used or under-powered; it will just do things a little more slowly.

Back-up Systems

Hard disks are more robust than floppies and can run marvellously for years without giving any trouble but when they do go down they can take an awful lot of data with them. The individual that fails to prepare for this is asking for trouble but the network that ignores this possibility is heading for disaster.

Back-up copies can be made on floppy disks but once you get beyond a few Megabytes this becomes very inconvenient. Even with the high-density $3^1/_2$" inch disks, a 20 Megabyte hard disk needs over a dozen to take a full back-up. You would need over 50 ordinary $5^1/_4$" floppies to do the same job. The alternative is to use a tape streamer. These high-speed, high-capacity cassette recorders are designed for the specific purpose of backing up hard disks. Back-up routines with these are much the same as with floppies. You should take a full back up on a weekly basis or after any major changes, such as the installation of a new package or the re-organisation of directories; and take regular back-ups of any files that have been updated. If the hard disk does go down, it can be recovered by restoring the last full back-up and the most recent partial copies.

A tape streamer must not be interrupted while backing up. This does not necessarily mean that the job can only be done after the day's work is over. If there are convenient quiet spells during the day, the disk could be temporarily closed to network users while the back-up is made.

Prices start at around £250 for a basic model that will take a full back-up of a 20 Megabyte drive in about twenty minutes; a 40 Megabyte back-up would take slightly over twice as long because you would have to change the tape cartridge in the middle. Larger and faster streamers can cost three or four times as much. You would normally only want one tape streamer in a network, even though there may be several hard disks, as it will receive only occasional use and can work across the network.

Print Servers and Printers

Much of what has been said about file servers applies equally to print servers. If a PC is to manage a printer and perform as a workstation, it must have a hard disk for the print queue. Disk space is not the problem here; if the queue is ever more than a few hundred kilobytes long, then the printer is being overloaded. Nor is it really a question of speed, for a floppy disk will be quick enough even for the fastest printer, though it would slow the PC down more when the file was being accessed. The crunch issue is that the network must be able to write a file into the print queue at all times, and that is not going to be convenient if the server only has floppy disk storage. The local user would be effectively barred from using one of the floppy drives, and each time the printing routines accessed the disk, normal processing would slow down. So, no matter how small the network, a floppy disk PC could only be used as a print server if it had no other functions.

An ordinary PC XT should be able to act as both server and workstation unless its local work involves heavy use of the hard disk or fast processing is essential. This would not be the case where its main use was for word processing, which makes few demands on either the disk or the processor, or for accounts work where the relevant files are likely to be held elsewhere.

Networks do not need special printers, though three points are worth bearing in mind. The first is that ideally all the printers used on the network should all be either Epson- or IBM-compatible. This is simply so that the printer control codes work in the same way on all machines. You will generally install application programs to work with a particular type of printer and it will be inconvenient if output cannot be diverted to others on the network should the normal printer be unavailable.

The second point is that mechanical printers tend to be noisy. If you are sitting next to a dot matrix or daisywheel printer, it is very hard not to be aware of it. The noise can be wearing, especially when the files that are being printed are nothing to do with you. A hood will reduce the level but, if you are buying a new printer for the network, it will be well worth while to spend a little extra for a quieter model. Some of the newer and better dot matrix printers are not too objectionable, and ink-jet machines produce little more than a hum and a whisper.

Lastly, a printer should be reasonably near its user. It doesn't matter if your files are stored on a hard disk two stories further up the building but it will be distinctly inconvenient if they are being printed up there!

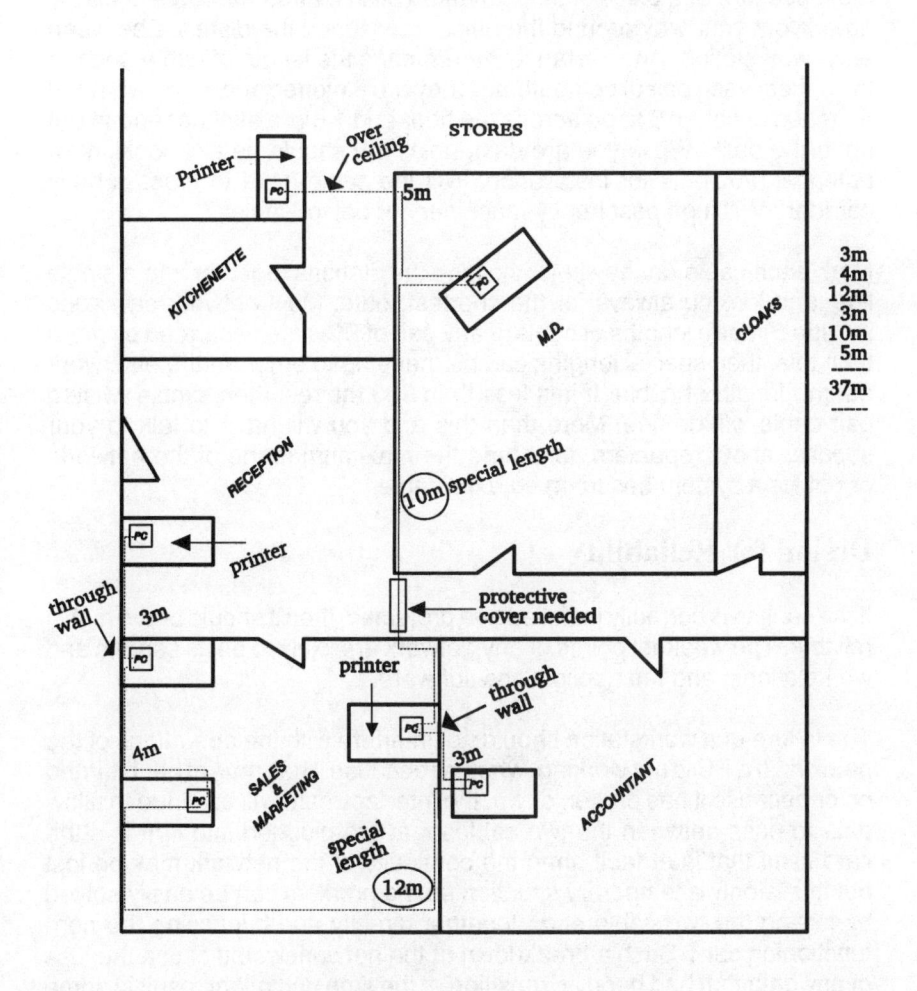

Figure 7.1 A sketch will help

Netware

Networking hardware and software has been covered at some length in earlier chapters. At this stage, you need to decide whether or not a good quality standard package, like MainLan, will do the job or whether you have special needs that require special solutions.

Size and spread is a key factor in the decision, so start by drawing up a sketch of the office(s), showing the probable positions of the PC's. A long tape measure or a piece of string marked off in metres will come in handy now. Work your way around the office, measuring the distance between each workstation. And 'distance' here means the length of cable needed to connect each pair of computers. If they are 3 metres apart, you will need 5 metres of cable: 3 to go across the floor and 1 more at either end to get up to the desk. While you are doing this, you should be also looking for potential problems for installation. Will the cable have to cross a busy corridor? Will it go past heavy machinery or power cables?

Mark each cable on the sketch, joining the stations together into a single line, and looking always for the shortest route. Most network packages include 5-metre lengths of cable; if any pair of PC's are separated by more than this, then special lengths can be made up to order. At the end, work out the length of cable. If it is less than 300 metres, then simple twisted pair cable will be fine. More than this and you will have to talk to your supplier about repeaters, to extend the maximum range of the network, or opt for a system based on co-axial cable.

Design for Reliability

If the cabling is correctly installed and protected, then it should prove highly reliable. The weakest points of any network are likely to be its servers and workstations, and the applications software.

The failure of a workstation should not interfere with the operations of the network. If a PC is not working, whether because it has not yet been turned on or because it has broken down, the interface card will continue to allow data to pass between the two cables that are plugged into it. If it is the card itself that is at fault, then the continuity of the network may be lost but this is only a temporary situation as the problem can be easily solved by joining the two cable ends together directly and bypassing the non-functioning card. Such a breakdown of the network would cause the loss of any data that had been in transition at the time and might result in some corruption of files. At worst, it might be necessary to go back to the previous day's back-up and re-enter any new data.

The failure of a file server should be no more damaging than - and almost as rare as - the breakdown of the network. However, recovery may take a little longer. It will be quickest in those cases where it is the PC which has failed, not the hard disk. Here, the disk could be transferred to another PC, its data checked and rebuilt from the back-ups if necessary.

In practice, hard disks are more likely to break down than PC's. When this happens, then ideally there should be enough spare capacity in the network to be able to transfer the work of the failed hard disk onto others. It will take a little while to re-organise the file storage and to reconfigure the network - perhaps a couple of hours - though the greatest danger in this sort of situation is to rush into it without thinking things through, and as a result create more problems. If the finances allow it, build redundancy into your network. Include an extra hard disk that is big enough to take over the complete load from any other disk and don't use it for any network file storage. It might be on the print server or be used for someone's local files. Should any file server break down, its functions can be transferred in total onto the surplus machine.

Where the network's PC's and hard disks are standard models from mainstream manufacturers, it should be possible to replace them within a few days. (Repair often takes longer as whole machines are generally easier to find than key components.) Buying all your equipment from a reputable supplier, and maintaining a good relationship with him, should help to ensure faster replacement.

Typical costings

The examples below are based on Amstrad 2000 series computers (with EGA colour monitors), Epson FX850 (Draft), Epson LQ850 (Letter Quality Dot Matrix) and Juki 6300 (Daisywheel) printers, Exerev 40 Mb tape streamers and either Sage or Torus networks. The printers are not the fastest in their ranges but have the best price/performance ratios. Prices shown are the normal retail ones at the time of writing. The total cost of the system will be reduced where existing hardware can be used but no allowance is made here for any multi-user software.

Hardware for the Network

4-User System

Workstation 1 / File Server		
PC 2086	30 Mb Hard Disk	£1150
Tape Streamer		£450
Workstation 2 / Print Server		
PC 2086	30 Mb Hard Disk	£1150
Letter Quality Printer		£480
Workstations 3 & 4		
2 x PC 2086	P Single Floppy @£850	£1700
Netware		
MainLan Starter + 2 Extensions		£800
	TOTAL	£5730

Notes: The network is probably coming up towards the limits of the file server's processing power, and the workstation may show some slowness at times of heavy disk activity. The next machine to be added to this network should be one with an 80286 or 80386 processor. This would then become the main file server.

The hard disk on workstation 2 is larger than necessary for print serving but would allow it to take over the disk-sharing functions of workstation 1 in the event of a failure.

Single floppy machines are perfectly adequate for normal workstation use. The disk drive is only needed for starting up and for the storage of private files.

If the only programs being used on the network are Sage Accounts (multi-user) and single-user software for word processing, spreadsheets and the like, then SageNet would be a viable alternative to MainLan. This would bring the netware cost down to around £550.

Hardware for the Network

8-User System

Workstation 1 / File Server		
PC 2286	40 Mb Hard Disk	£1500
Tape Streamer		£450
Workstation 2 / Print Server		
PC 2086	30 Mb Hard Disk	£1150
Draft Printer		£330
Workstation 3 / Print Server		
PC 2086	30 Mb Hard Disk	£1150
Daisywheel Printer		£360
Workstations 4 to 8		
5 x PC 2086	Single Floppy @£850	£4250
Netware		
MainLan Starter + 6 Extensions		£1600
2 extra long cable lengths		£60
	TOTAL	£10850

Notes: It should be possible to add another two or three workstations to this network without upgrading the servers. Cost per additional station is £1050, including netware.

The substitution of an Amstrad 2386 as the main file server would improve the efficiency of the network and lift the total cost by £1300.

In practice this network should cost considerably less than £10,000 to set up as there will almost certainly be a number of PC's, hard disks and printers already in use. Deduct as appropriate.

Hardware for the Network

16-User System

Workstation 1 / File Server (Data)
PC 2386	65 Mb Hard Disk	£2800
Tape Streamer		£450

Workstation 2 / File Server (Programs)
PC 2386	65 Mb Hard Disk	£2800
Tape Streamer		£450

Workstation 3 / Print Server
PC 2286	40 Mb Hard Disk	£1500
Letter Quality Printer		£480

Workstation 4 / Print Server
PC 2286	40 Mb Hard Disk	£1500
Draft Printer		£330

Workstation 5 / Print Server
PC 2086	30 Mb Hard Disk	£1150
Daisywheel Printer		£360

Workstations 6 to 16
11 x PC 2086 Single Floppy @£850	£9350
Local / Occasional Use Printer	£330
Local / Occasional Use Hard Disk	£300

Netware
MainLan Starter + 14 Extensions	£3200
Allowance for extra cable	£180

TOTAL £25180

Notes: Allowance has been made for an additional printer and hard disk, mainly intended for local use, but which could be pressed into the service of the network in times of need.

There is probably more storage capacity than is needed - about 270 Megabytes in total. The redundancy could prove worthwhile in the event of the breakdown of any of the hard disk machines.

A second tape streamer has been added here. It is not strictly essential but its presence will make backing up quicker, more convenient and therefore more likely to be done regularly.

Hardware for the Network

In a normal office environment, MainLan should give very satisfactory performance, reliable and fast enough for all purposes. Where special conditions exist - the network is spread over a very wide area, cables have to pass heavy electrical equipment or there is a need for very high speed of data transfer - then an Ethernet-based system, such as Torus Tapestry, might be needed. With Ethernet interface cards costing £400 each and software averaging around £300 per station, as opposed to a MainLan cost of about £200 per PC, this would add almost £5000 to the overall bill.

8

The Office and the System

Installing a network into an office is not just a matter of wiring up the hardware and setting up the disk- and printer-sharing. New multi-user software must be brought into operation and staff must be trained and allocated roles within the network. It can all add up to a lot of work but fortunately networks have this very attractive feature of lending themselves naturally to a gradual installation. It is not necessary to cable all the computers together at once or to switch immediately to multi-user software. You won't get the full benefits of the network until the process is complete but at least you can take it at your own pace.

What must be done at the very beginning is to think through the integration of the network into the office's working practices. At the most basic level, who is going to take responsibility for it? But there is a lot more to it than that and it may be helpful to perform a breakdown of chores and responsibilities, and allocate them as necessary, so that people can see what will be expected of them. This should be done before any final decisions are taken on either hardware or software. Those who will be directly affected should be allowed to make their contribution to the decision-making.

Network Management

Long term, requiring working understanding of DOS, netware and applications programs.

- Selection, installation and maintenance of network, computers and peripherals.

- Selection and installation of applications programs.

- Staff training.

Daily, straightforward man-management.

- Ensuring file and print servers are properly staffed at all times.

While it will generally be best to have a single network manager with overall responsibility, most of the long-term decisions should only be taken after extensive consultation. This applies particularly to the choice of applications software, especially where there are a variety of single-user programs of the same type currently in use. If different people are word processing with WordStar, DisplayWrite, MicroSoft Word and Word Perfect, they may be able to continue using them for their individual work but they should agree on a common program for common work, and it is logical to opt for that which requires least training for the fewest people. It is perhaps a reflection of the move towards networking that an increasing number of programs are now appearing that allow the users to customise the command structure. Borland's Sprint, for example, can be made to mimic all of the four word processors mentioned above, and more.

A network will require a certain amount of routine supervision and occasional maintenance, so that potential problems can be identified and nipped in the bud. Some jobs are network-wide and fall into the domain of the network manager; others are best handled by those with responsibility for the print and file servers.

File Server

Long term, requires working understanding of network.

- Allocation of passwords and space on shared disks.

Daily routine.

- Ensuring server is operational during working hours.
- Backing up all files on regular basis.

Print Server

Continual, requires understanding of printer and network print facilities.

- Ensuring server is operational during working hours.
- Coping with paper jams and other down-times.

Continual, routine.

- Ensuring supplies of paper and ink.
- Collecting outputs.

Users

Daily, requires basic knowledge of DOS and disk sharing facilities.

- Organisation of own directories on shared disks.
- Back-ups of private files on local disks.

Some of these tasks and responsibilities will be obvious; others are more complex and may best be seen in the context of setting up and running a network.

Installation and Management

9

Installing the Network

In the simplest cases, the installation of the network will require no more than limited technical knowledge and mechanical ability. With SageNet or MainLan in a compact office, the hardware installation consists of fitting the interface cards into the expansion slots of the computers and fixing the cable with cable clips or through plastic trunking. Setting up the network software requires no more than the ability to follow the step by step instructions of the installation program.

Where co-axial cable is being used, or special lengths have to be made up on site, or if any of the other aspects of setting up require specialist knowledge, it would be as well to arrange for the supplier to carry out the installation.

Installing the Network

Stage 1 - The Trial Network

Start with a minimal network: a file server and a workstation. Fit the interface cards and plug in the cable but don't fasten the cable down yet. Run the installation program on both machines then check that the network software is running properly. On MainLan, the 'Who' Utility will tell you whether or not the computers are on the network. Test as many of the other functions as you can at this stage; it's an ideal way of finding out about it. Bring a printer into your network, either by connecting it to one of the two linked machines or by adding another PC along with the printer. Install, or reconfigure, the print server and test it by printing a short text file across the network.

Stage 2 - Applications Software

Once you have a basic hardware set up it's time to make a start on the applications software. There is no point in linking in all the rest of the computers until you have something for them to do! It is worth making a few general points about software at this stage; we will return to look at different applications in later chapters.

Begin with the new multi-user programs - they are presumably the main reason for the network - and tackle then one at a time. Install them and create some test files that will allow you to check them out thoroughly. With a good quality network, there should be no problems with purpose-built multi-user software but don't skimp the time spent on testing. It could prevent problems later and during the process you will learn a lot about the program.

Single-User Software

Where there are single-user programs already on the hard disk, they should be checked carefully to ensure that they can be used fully and safely. Some may not fit into the available memory, particularly on servers where the network software needs more space. Others may have been coded so that they will only work on the machine in which they are installed.

There is a further problem that is most likely to be noticed with word-processing programs, though it will crop up elsewhere. Many applications allow their users to write in their own default settings. With word processing these are for things like the width of margins, page lengths and the presence of headers; other programs let you specify screen colours and the way the function keys behave. This is a great convenience where the single-user software has a single user but could be less convenient where there are several users.

Data Integrity

Even where programs do run, there is always a potential problem of data integrity. The files from single-user software should never be stored or used communally. If they are, there will be times when two people try to update the same file at the same time. When this happens, then either the data will become corrupted or when the second user saves the file it will overwrite the first person's new version, wiping out any work that has been done. You may also find that some of your programs produce temporary files automatically while carrying out certain functions and that these files normally have standard names supplied by the software. If a database program creates such files when sorting or a word processor when moving large blocks of text, what happens if two people are using the same program at the same time? The answer is that one or both users will find that their data has been corrupted or overwritten.

Copyright

With all single-user software there is also a potential copyright problem, so that even though you can use a program, you may not be able to use it legally. Most software is sold under a licence agreement, so that what you buy is not the program itself but the right to use it under certain conditions. With single-user programs, that will normally mean that you may make one copy, for security purposes. Sometimes the licence will state clearly that the program may only be used on one machine; sometimes this will be implicit in the one-copy restriction.

The legal position on network use is not always clear. If a program is installed on a user's local hard disk, or in their private directory on a shared disk, and used only by that person, this would seem to be well within the terms of a normal single-user licence. If it is installed in an open shared directory and used willy-nilly by everyone on the network, then that would seem to be a clear abuse of the licence. In between is a grey area, where the program is generally available but in practice only used by one person at a time - perhaps because it has a very specific purpose, or perhaps because it is used very little. If the software is only used by one person at a time, does it make a difference if the person goes to the software, on a certain machine, or if the software comes to the person, across the network?

Stage 3 - User Training

In some cases this may be better left until after the cabling up but it will usually be a good idea to give staff basic training in the use of the network before the equipment appears on their desks. At the very least, the ordinary workstation users must know how to access and use the relevant network facilities; how to connect to shared disks so that programs may be run, files loaded and saved; and how to divert output to remote printers. Those responsible for servers must have the opportunity to practice their roles, and to make the errors of inexperience without other people being affected.

Stage 4 - Cabling Up

Double-check the physical layout of the hardware before you fix the cables into place. Are the PC's - and perhaps even more crucially the printers - in the right places? Set the equipment out and ask for comments from the people who will use it. It might even be an idea to install the network, with loose cables, and run it on a trial basis for a few days. It may prove to be more convenient to attach a printer to a different machine, or that a PC needs to be relocated elsewhere in the office.

Whether permanent or temporary, the installation should be done one station at a time, making sure that each is on the network and functioning properly before moving on to the next.

As the order in which machines are connected is irrelevant to the operation of the network, keeping the cable run as secure and as short as possible are the only things that matter. Cables tucked under carpets won't last very long and trailing leads are an obvious hazard to avoid, which is why a temporary set-up must be very temporary. Plastic trunking will provide a reasonable level of protection from physical damage and is not unsightly if fitted properly.

Shielded twisted pair cable, such as that used in MainLan, and co-axial cable can tolerate a moderate level of electromagnetic interference - the sort produced by mains wiring and light electrical equipment. Where a cable has to run through a workshop or other harsh environment, then the normal shielding may not be adequate. In these or any other cases where you are in any way unsure about the installation, put your problems in the hands of a reputable dealer.

Installing the Network

Maintenance and Trouble-Shooting

The failure of a PC will be a nuisance, especially if it is a file or print server, but it will rarely affect the rest of the network. But if a cable length or interface card develops a fault, this could well show up in the failure of the whole network. So if a problem does occur, the first job is to track it down. Some network packages, like MainLan, will include a diagnostic utility that will do much of the work for you but on any bus structure it's quite easy to isolate a fault.

Start by turning off all the stations. Then take the terminator plug from one end of the network and use it to close off the network after the first pair of machines at the other end. Perform the normal network start-up on those stations and check that all is well.

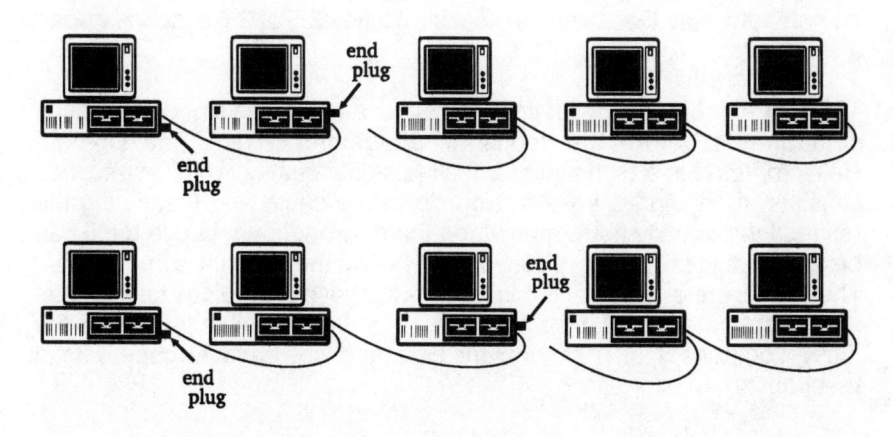

Figure 9.1 Checking the network in stages

Reconnect the third station and move the end plug into this PC. Start it up and test. Continue in this way, gradually extending the working net until you reach the point where it fails. Check the connections carefully and, if they seem good, then test the components by replacing one at a time. Reconnecting the PC one place further back up the working net is a good first move. If it works there, then the problem is almost certainly in the next length of cable. If it doesn't, then swap its interface card with another one that you know works and try again. Should you still have no joy, then the fault would appear to lie with the PC itself. Double check by returning to the original cable and card and a different PC.

105

Installing the Network

Where replacement cable, cards or computers cannot be obtained immediately, bypass the failure and restore the rest of the network. A faulty card or PC can be cut out of the network by the simple expedient of plugging together the two cables that had been attached to that station. A faulty cable is more problematic and a spare length of cable may be worth having, though this is the least likely component to fail.

In practice, a network breakdown will probably be the end result of a gradual process. Cable and interfaces can both degrade over time, and any loss of function will not be obvious to the users. If data is corrupted in transmission, the errors will normally be spotted and handled by the network software, so that the only signs of impending failure will be a slowing down of transmissions. The poorer the quality of the signals, the more often the same packet of data will have to be sent across the net. But speeds are always relative and variations are frequently beyond human detection. Does anyone notice if it takes 2.5 or 2.6 seconds to load a file?

There are methods of testing networks and identifying deteriorating components before they collapse altogether. TDR (Time Domain Reflectometry) is a technique for testing signal quality, which in essence consists of sending a transmission down the cable and measuring the result. It is normally performed when the network is not in use but it can be done within an overall quality analysis while the network is operational. The results are digitised and compared with those of previous tests to give early warning of developing problems. It is then possible to replace the faulty component at a convenient time and not have to cope with a breakdown.

At the moment such test procedures are probably too specialised and expensive to be considered worthwhile on a normal small- to medium-sized commercial network; the cost of a breakdown could be less than the cost of predicting and preventing it. But it seems to be in the nature of computing for things to become cheaper, and more effective, all the time. Watch out for predictor utilities, and use them if you can.

10

Network Management

The File Server

Passwords and security

The security and the integrity of data and program files is vital. The first step in ensuring this is to restrict access as far as possible - but without impairing people's ability to get on with their jobs!

For program files, the most reasonable solution is to locate all common programs within one super directory; it can be sub-divided into separate directories for each application. There is probably little point in protecting this by a password but it is worthwhile using the DOS command 'ATTRIB +R' to make these files read only, and so protect them from accidental erasure. It won't prevent a determined effort to corrupt them but, even if

Network Management

that happens, there will be no permanent loss. The programs can always be restored from the back-ups or from their original master disks.

In the same way, all common files should be located within one large directory but this should be password protected - and the password must be changed on a regular basis or when there is any hint that an unauthorised person may have learnt it. This is essential even where the applications software has its own passwords to control access to sensitive files. The passwords at the network level will make it far more difficult to erase files. They will not guarantee complete security but, combined with regular back-ups, the system will be protected from any major loss of data.

In the example network in Chapter 5, each of the users had separate directories for each application. This may well have made their life easier; once the connection has been made to the named area, the right files are available without having to change directory. Against that, with a maximum of 16 shared areas per disk (MainLan), the system can soon run out of areas. A more effective method would be to allocate each user his or her own directory, which can then be subdivided for applications. From the user's point of view, it will take only a single password to get to their files, though switching to the relevant sub-directory will be necessary.

The overall structure might follow that shown in Figure 10.1.

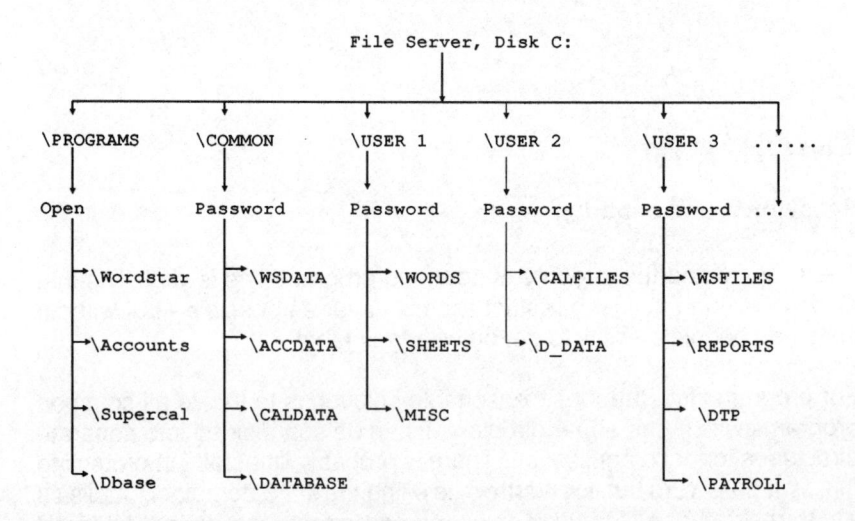

```
                        File Server, Disk C:
                                 |
    ┌────────────┬──────────┬────┴────┬─────────┬─────────┬──────
    ▼            ▼          ▼         ▼         ▼
\PROGRAMS    \COMMON     \USER 1   \USER 2   \USER 3    ......
    |            |          |         |         |
   Open      Password   Password  Password  Password    ....

   ┌─\Wordstar  ┌─\WSDATA  ┌─\WORDS   ┌─\CALFILES  ┌─\WSFILES
   │            │          │          │            │
   ├─\Accounts  ├─\ACCDATA ├─\SHEETS  └─\D_DATA    ├─\REPORTS
   │            │          │                       │
   ├─\Supercal  ├─\CALDATA └─\MISC                 ├─\DTP
   │            │                                   │
   └─\Dbase     └─\DATABASE                        └─\PAYROLL
```

Figure 10.1 Directory structure with passwords

Network Management

As has been mentioned already, hard disks have a tendency to become clogged up with unnecessary files: copies of old correspondence and reports, 'temporary' sorted files from databases, programs that are no longer used. It is a tendency that should be fought rigorously, partly because it is a waste of space - though hard disk space is cheap nowadays at around 1.5p per kilobyte - but mainly because the things that matter can become submerged in the clutter. Those looking after the file servers should trawl regularly through the \PROGRAMS and \COMMON directories and any other areas for which they are directly responsible; and they should encourage sharing users to do the same in their own areas. Unwanted files can either be deleted or transferred to floppy disk or tape streamer for permanent storage.

Backing up files

The person responsible for the file server should also be responsible for backing up all the files on the disk, whether common or belonging to individual users. Back-ups must be done regularly - it needn't take long. While a full back-up could occupy the better part of half an hour, daily back-ups can be done in a few minutes. This can be managed by using a tape streamer and one of the commercial utilities (Clip from Keele Codes is an excellent example), which keeps a log of back-ups and enables you to save only those files that have been altered since the previous operation.

It is important to establish a routine and to let all users know when back-ups will be taken. The frequency and nature of such back-ups must vary with the work being done but a timetable for a typical office might well follow that shown in Figure 10.2.

5.00	Friday	-	Full disk back-up	
5.15	Monday	-	Partial A	
5.15	Tuesday	-	Partial B	
5.15	Wednesday	-	Partial C	
1.00	Thursday	-	Partial D	(Thursday mornings always busy)
5.15	Thursday	-	Partial E	

Figure 10.2 The back-up schedule

Should a crash occur on a Wednesday afternoon, for example, the recovery route would be to restore the disk from the previous Friday's full back-up then partial back-ups A and B. Any editing or data entry that had been done during Wednesday would have to be redone.

In those offices where there is a great deal of new data being typed in all the time, back-ups could be taken two or three times a day. It is possible to overdo this, for the disk must be taken off the network during back-ups. The efficient disk manager will aim to strike a balance between security and convenience. Given that the mean time between failure of a good quality hard disk is in the region of two years, how many working hours would it take to re-enter data lost in a crash, and how does this compare with the time spent on backing up? A worked example may help to put this into context.

Firstly, data rarely takes as long to enter the second time; there will usually be printer summaries, copies of invoices, draft letters and such to work from. So, if there are six people on the network, all typing for most of the time, a full day's work of 42 man-hours (6 x 7) could probably be put back in less than 20 hours.

If the back-up routine is as given above, and it takes 30 minutes for a full and 10 minutes for a partial back-up, the total time for the week is around one and a half hours. Assuming a hardware failure every two years and a crash from other causes - power failure or human error - once a year, the average time between crashes will be around thirty weeks. That gives about 45 hours back-up time to balance against 20 hours' lost work, which is probably reasonable. Backing up is an undemanding process during which other small chores can be done; replacing lost work is far more stressful and frustrating.

You can calculate the economics of this far more closely if you can cost people's time accurately and get realistic estimates of the frequencies of failures. That may not be possible until the network has been in operation for some while.

Managing the Print Server

Of all the hardware on the network, the printers are the ones which will require the most regular attention. If nothing else, they need a steady supply of consumables - paper and ink, in its various forms. At its simplest, being responsible for the printer may mean nothing more than making sure that there is plenty of paper available and that the print is still black enough. A quick look in the box or in the feed tray and running the self-test as the printer is turned on may be all that is needed. At its worst, a printer may need almost constant attention, though this will be more of a reflection on the other users, rather on the machine itself.

If the firm uses special forms and headed paper for its invoices, credit notes, delivery notes, memos, letters and the like, and all of these have to be run off by the same printer, who is responsible for ensuring that the right paper is there at the right time? Probably the only satisfactory solution in this situation is to have one person in charge of the printer, with this working as a local device. Files can then be sent, along with paper requests, via the mail facility to the printing clerk, who can change paper types before printing directly.

Some programs generate printed output automatically; some accounts packages, for example, produce a paper summary whenever certain update routines are run. As this happens without any prompting by the user there is no opportunity to control the printing at the time. This can create problems, particularly if special paper is needed. The best solution is to use a PC with a local printer but, where this is not possible, other network users must be informed beforehand and requested not to use the selected printer. If they do send files, the printouts will be mixed with, and possibly corrupted by, the sporadic automatic output.

Other user-created problems are less obvious. Someone selecting a special print mode or setting unusual margins at the start of a file may forget to change back to normal at the end. People may not appear immediately to collect their printing and will then have to hunt through a pile of assorted outputs later in the day. Both of these can be solved readily by the addition of a header page to every file. This can be done automatically and can reset normal typefaces and layouts as well as identifying the owner. Having someone at hand to collate and stack output will also help.

Those annoying people who crank up the paper by hand, rather than using a form feed, are more difficult to deal with, and a misaligned page start can turn a stack of paper into bin-fodder in very little time. Training will help, as will - once again - having someone around who understands the printer and keeps a beady eye on it.

Network Management

On Being a Network User

At the end of the day, good network practices are largely a matter of common sense and thought for others. When people are working on their own individual computers, their sloppy habits may lower their own efficiency but will have only limited affects on others in the office. On a network, sloppy habits affect everybody.

If hard-disk storage is in short supply, then users must be economical in their use of it. Even a memory-rich network will run into problems eventually if people store all files without thought to why or for how long. And in the event of a hard-disk failure, any network could find itself short of storage for a little while at least. Clearing out unwanted files will also make it easier to find those files that you do want. A regular cull is always advisable and often essential.

A little consideration goes a long way with the printing too. If you are sending a hefty report down to the daisywheel, it could tie up the printer for quite a while. It only takes a moment to check if other users have urgent printing that they want to squeeze in first. Collecting output promptly and leaving the printer ready for the next user are all part of good network practice.

Where a person is working at a combined server and workstation, additional rules apply. The most obvious is to make sure that the machine is up and running at all times when it might be needed but there is more to that than just turning on at the start of the day. It is vital that they should not use any program that might cause the PC to crash, and the `[Ctrl]-[Alt]-[Del]` reboot is no longer an acceptable method of getting out of a messy situation. DIY and any cheap and cheerful software should be banned from a dual-purpose station, and memory-resident programs must be used with care.

The plus side for every network user will be access to a greater range of facilities, better communications and the improved efficiency and productivity that comes from sharing data and pooling effort.

Networks and Application Software

11

Sharing Data

All true multi-user software has to solve the same major problem of how to allow users to share data safely and efficiently. An indifferent solution may not matter much with word processing, spreadsheets and the like, where most users are working on their own individual files for most of the time. But with company-wide databases or integrated accounting packages, effective data sharing is the key to its success, for here most users will be working on the same files most of the time. People must be able to gain access to and change the same data at any time. Let's see what problems are raised by this and how they can be solved.

Two people are working on the accounts, one making out invoices and updating the customers' files, another recording payments - and updating the customers' files. If they were using a paper-based system what would happen? Obviously it will depend upon the nature of the system, but basically they are both going to be accessing the same ledgers or filing cabinets on and off continually (unless they both turn the updating over to a third person, which is a different situation). There will be times when they will get in each other's way and one will have to stand aside for a moment until the right drawer or ledger can be reached. Assume that a

Sharing Data

significant proportion of their output goes to one major customer and the delays become more marked, for they cannot both update the same record simultaneously.

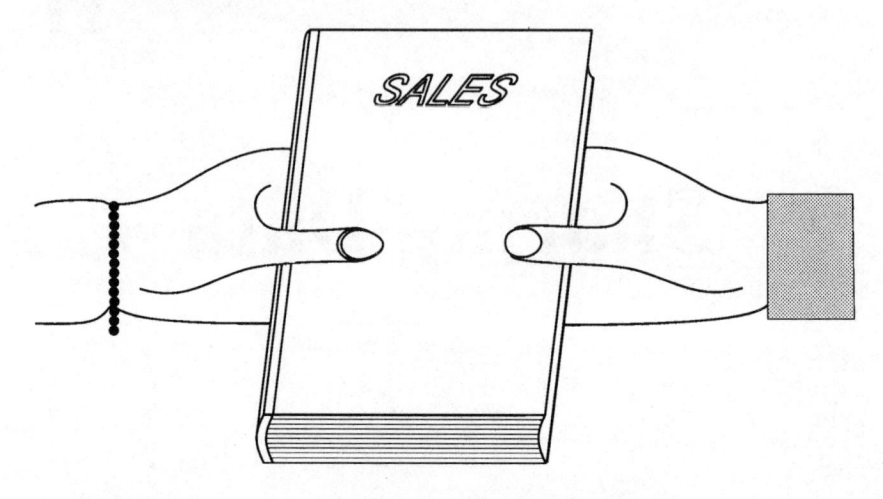

Figure 11.1 One at a time, please!

Now add a third person whose job is to check those files before sending out overdue notices. How often will unnecessary reminders be sent, simply because the payment clerk could not clear the debt from the record as it was on the credit controller's desk at the time?

The system is inefficient - which is why more and more business have been turning to computers for their accounting - but it is safe, which is one reason why there are still many using paper. As long as people don't wander off with files and forget to return them the relevant data is always there and reasonably up to date.

Maintaining the integrity of data in a computer system is more complicated because the files do not have simple physical presence and it is quite possible for several copies of a file to be in existence simultaneously. The invoicing clerk could call up a customer's record and add in the new debt, while the payment clerk has the same record on his screen and is typing in the receipts. What happens next depends upon who finishes first. If the invoicing clerk is first, the new debt will be erased when the payment clerk saves her version of the account on top of the last one; if it goes the other way then the record of payment will have been lost. Whatever else it does, the software must prevent two people from working on the same data at the same time.

Sharing Data

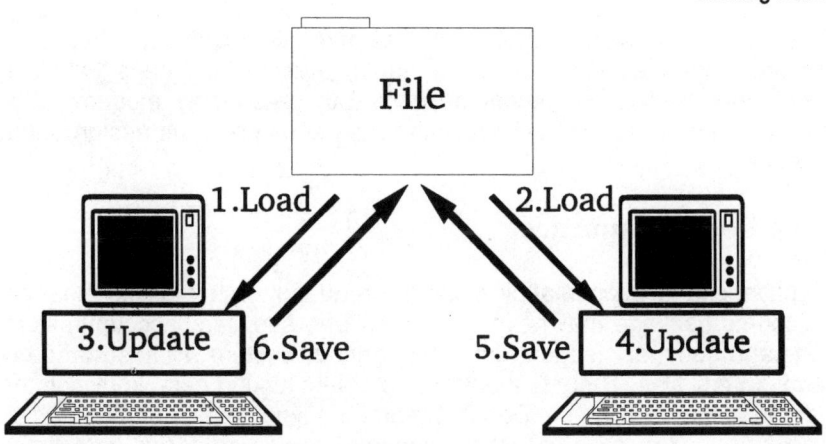

Figure 11.2 Whose copy is saved?

File and Record Locking

There are two levels at which you can control access in a computerised system - the *file* and the *record*. Restricting access to a file is akin to having a single ledger, so that if someone is updating the account of a customer, no-one else can get at the accounts of any other customer. Working at record level is more like using a filing cabinet. Several people can get at different customers' accounts simultaneously, and the conflicts only arise when two or more want to work on the same account. Clearly, record-locking will create fewer delays than file-locking.

Whether at file or record level, the locks can be applied in two different ways. Other users can be denied all access to data which is already being processed or they can be allowed to read but not write. The value of this facility will depend upon the use to which the data is being put and the level of the locking. If a file is locked whenever someone updates a record, then being able to at least read the file could well be useful - even though one of the records will presumably no longer be accurate. If it is only the individual record that is locked, then being able to read data which is in the process of being changed may be less valuable.

In more sophisticated software a user will be informed of any changes that are being made, and some applications programs even update the screens automatically if they contain data that has been edited since first displayed. This may not happen often with individual records but where a person is examining summary reports screen updating will ensure the up-to-the-minute accuracy of information.

Sharing Data

MS-DOS, in versions 3.0 and later, is perfectly capable of supporting record-locking, either read-only or total. In practice this means that it can be managed on any decent network with reasonably modern PC's. Whether file- or record-locking is used depends upon the design of the software.

The Deadly Embrace

Database and accountancy systems frequently use multiple files. An accounts package may have customers' and suppliers' accounts, stock lists and summary ledgers; an estate agency system will keep property and buyers' files. There is a potential problem lurking here, known in the jargon of the trade as the Deadly Embrace. If you have operations which require two files to be updated, sometimes in one order and sometimes in the other, it is possible for both to become inextricably locked. An example might help.

In processing a purchase order, the accountancy software might reasonably begin at the supplier's file, to get the necessary details of the firm, then go on to write a note of the order into the stock file. The routine locks the supplier's file, but must access the stock file before it can finish. This same software might process the receipts of goods by first recording them in the stock file and then updating the supplier's file. It will thereby have locked the stock file but must gain access to the supplier's file before it can finish. Both routines are waiting for each other. This is the Deadly Embrace.

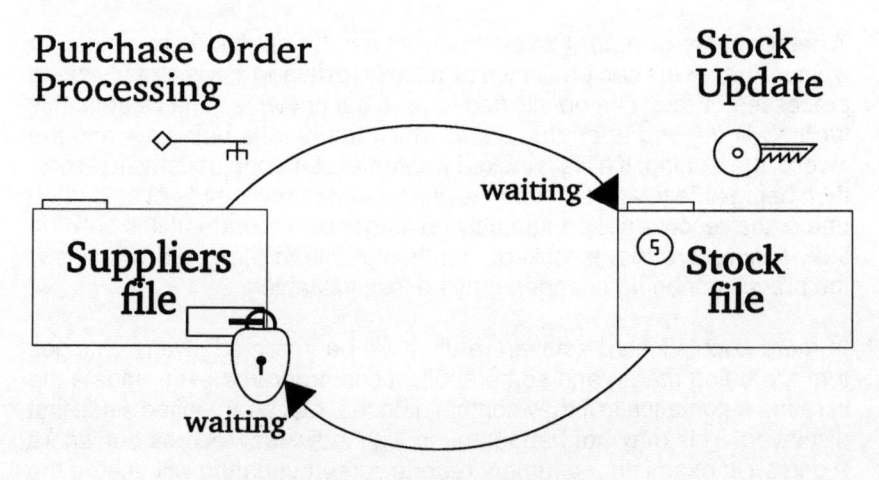

Figure 11.3 The Deadly Embrace

It would be a poorly designed accounts system if it did work this way but there are other times when the logic of the interactions are not so clearly visible. In practice, the problem is more likely to occur in a relational database system that supports interactive files and where the application may have been programmed by someone without the necessary level of expertise. There are a number of solutions; the simplest is to abort the operation if the second file is locked, release the lock on the first file and start again after a random wait. There is nothing in the nature of networks or MS-DOS which makes the deadly embrace inevitable.

One last point on data sharing before we move on to look at software for the network. If the use of a database is the main application for the network, and raw processing power is less important, then a multi-user system may sometimes be more efficient than a network. This might be the case, for example, in an estate agency where most of the work consists of reading and occasionally updating property files. Such a firm may find that they get a better performance from a minicomputer or a high-powered micro and a set of dumb terminals, than they would from a net of PC's (see Appendix A, the Multi-user Alternative).

12

Suitable Software

At the time of writing, networks are just beginning to be taken up by small businesses and, though there is a reasonable range of suitable multi-user software around, the real explosion has yet to happen. As networks come into widespread use over the next few years, there is bound to be a massive increase in the number and variety of suitable applications programs.

Database Management Systems

With *dBASE II* and *dBASE III* the applications programs may be shared on the network but not the data, unless the programs have been rewritten to implement locks on files and records. Even then the result may not be satisfactory as the programs tend to run noticeably slower on networks. If you are a dBASE user, upgrade to *dBASE III Plus*, which is designed for networks; or switch to *Foxbase* or *Clipper*, which work in the same way but run faster.

Another high-speed network solution is the *dBFast* compiler. This implements MS-DOS record locks but also has another method for

Suitable Software

avoiding the problems caused by simultaneous updating. Before an edited record is written back to the disk the program re-reads the data on disk and compares it with the previous version. If it has been changed, then the update is aborted and the user is informed.

Sage's new *Retrieve III* is for single users only but its big brother, *Retrieve IV*, is for network use. The two are compatible, so any files created now under III can be used with IV when you go over to a network. Quite apart from being a good, user-friendly package (or at least, user-friendly for a database), this has the added advantage for Sage MainLan users of being highly tested and guaranteed safe on the network. Full file and record locks are implemented and access to files is restricted by passwords.

Accounting Systems

These can, of course, be generated by any good database software but if the firm prefers the simplicity of a special-purpose accountancy package there is plenty of choice. All of the mainstream software - Pegasus, Sun Account, Sage Financial Controller, MAP and TAS, amongst others - is now available in multi-user versions, with file and record-locking as standard. All of these will be able to take the files created by the single-user versions of the same software, giving a simple, trouble-free upgrade path.

Where the only multi-user software to be used on the network is for accounting, then the combination of Financial Controller or Accountant and SageNet offers a low-cost, reliable solution.

Spreadsheets

Spreadsheet files are more typically created and used by individuals, rather than being company-wide resources, so the ability to allow simultaneous access by several users may not be important. It may be enough to be able to run the spreadsheet programs across the net. Where a number of people have a contribution to make to a single file, it could be done sequentially by transferring the file from one user to another in turn.

Lotus 1-2-3 2.01, as a single-user program, can be used on a network, providing you purchase additional key disks for each user; if the disk is not present in the A: drive, the software won't work. As there is no form of file-locking, simultaneous access would corrupt the data, so it is important to have a separate storage area for each person's files. The multi-user version can be used safely, though again the copy-protection means that a key disk is needed for every user. Key disks represent an additional expense on an already expensive program and they can be an irritant. Where the spreadsheet receives only occasional use by some people it seems a little unnecessary to buy key disks for everyone but, if you rely on a shared pool of disks, it's a fair bet that they will get scattered around the office and never be at hand when wanted. Version 3, when it appears, will not have this copy-protection.

With *SuperCalc 2 and 3*, the programs can be run across the network without any bother but, as these are single-user versions, each person's files must be kept separate. *SuperCalc 4 and 5* are both fully-fledged multi-user versions. As they can run Lotus-derived spreadsheets and use Lotus-style commands and macros, a switch from 1-2-3 to SuperCalc 4 or 5 is a convenient upgrade path for disenchanted Lotus users. Borland's *Quattro* offers the same 1-2-3 compatibility and the single-user version can be used across the network. If you want to stay with Sage products on a MainLan network, then their *PC Planner Release 2* is a low-cost, 1-2-3 compatible, multi-user spreadsheet.

Multiplan 3 and 4 are the network versions of this old favourite, though now rather over-shadowed by MicroSoft's other spreadsheet (and more) package, *Excel*.

Word Processing

Though word processing is intrinsically a solitary activity - even more so than spreadsheeting - there are considerable advantages to be had by working on a net. The most obvious of these is that people can share printers conveniently. This can reduce costs, for a single printer can serve a number of users; and it can offer alternative outputs: a quick draft copy for the internal files and a slow high-quality print for the customer. Such a level of sharing would be quite impractical with a set of separate PC's, where people would have to carry files around on disks and wait for access to the printer. Another benefit that should be apparent from the outset is that networked access to database files will make mail-shots, circulars, standard reminder letters and the like much easier to produce.

If a document has to be circulated either before or after publication, whether it is a letter for one person to check or a memo for general distribution, this can be handled through a network's mailing facility. This will reduce the amount of paper floating across people's desks, but will also make sure that the documents reach the right people.

Suitable Software

Boilerplates

Lastly, networking will enable a firm to improve and standardise its word-processed output through the use of boilerplates. If a stock of standard document formats and paragraphs are held in a common area all users will be able to draw on these and tailor them for specific needs. Sets of ready-written boilerplates can be bought off the shelf or can be created within the firm; acknowledgements, quotations, reminders and announcements can then be produced quickly and to a common house style.

The user begins work on a document by copying - not loading - the relevant boilerplate or by merging it into the new document file. Unwanted paragraphs can then be trimmed out and personal details added. Other standard blocks could also be merged in later, as needed. A network is not essential for this, as it is quite feasible to distribute copies of the boilerplate disk to all users, but adaptations and additions are more difficult to manage with separate PC's. With a network, any updating of the boilerplate library will be instantly available to all.

A point to remember about word-processing software is that it is almost always installed to meet the specific requirements of its user. Some of the customising will be valid company-wide; if you are aiming for a house style through the use of boilerplates, then margins, headers and footers and other aspects of layout should also be standardised. Other parts of the installation may be different for each user. What type is the default printer? Where are personal dictionaries stored for the spelling checker and what are they called? If there are no variations, then a centrally installed, single-user program may be adequate; but if individual requirements differ, then you will either need true multi-user software or a package which allows you to store the configuration separately from the main program.

Note also that some word-processing packages will automatically produce temporary files when they are moving large blocks of text or when the file grows beyond the limits of the internal memory. Single-user versions of these cannot be used on a network unless they allow you to specify where to store those temporary files.

Word Version 3 is designed for use on a network, though restricted to a maximum of five users at any one time. Extensions can be bought if greater access is needed.

Suitable Software

Word Perfect and *WordStar Professional* can both be installed as multi-user systems and will support separate directories for individual users.

Volkswriter Deluxe, another great favourite, can be run on a network as it can be configured so that its temporary files and personal dictionaries are stored separately.

WordStar Professional, now in version 5, is suitable for network use, as well as being probably the slickest and most comprehensive word-processing package around.

Communications

13

Electronic Memos and Networked Communications

In a small office, where people are within sight and sound of each other a network's mail facilities are likely to be of very limited use and may even impair rather than improve communications. A message sent across the net will generally take longer to type than it would to say; it may not be read immediately; it may be imperfectly understood; and, if in any way confidential, sensitive or potentially embarrassing for someone, should perhaps not have been committed to any kind of permanent medium. If you can walk across to the other person's desk and talk to them directly it will generally be quicker and frequently more effective than electronic mail.

There are a few exceptions. The mail can be useful for passing a note to someone who is in a meeting or on the 'phone; it's less intrusive or distracting than turning up at their desk. If the person at the file server is about to do the daily back-up then flashing 'Back-up in five minutes' on the other users' screens will be a good way of getting the message round. Likewise, a printer's minder might use the mail to alert people before taking the printer off the network or changing its paper type. If the other users are not concerned, then they can ignore the message without having to break off from their work to reply to a spoken notification.

Mail, Memos and Calls

Once the network spreads beyond a single office, electronic mail becomes of more value for internal communications. As a rule of thumb, if the firm currently uses memos or a telephone system then the mail will be useful, for it can replace both of these to some extent.

Looking at mail in place of memos, the most significant limiting factor is probably the typing skills of the users; office efficiency will not be improved by insisting that even the two-fingered typists send their messages by mail. And even where all users can type proficiently, the mail may prove a mixed blessing. In the early days after the installation of the network, there could well be a good deal of unnecessary traffic as people play with the mail, and the novelty wears off slowly for some. The wise network manager will keep an eye open for time-wasting, from whatever cause, and make sure that the facility is used for the benefit of the office.

But let's not be too negative. Electronic mail does have some clear advantages over the paper memo. It is transmitted instantaneously, requires no-one to carry it round, and is probably easier to manage. All decent networking packages have comprehensive routines for announcing the arrival of new mail, for storing it, answering directly or passing messages on to others. In MainLan, for example, messages are held conveniently in a neatly organised mailbox on disk, rather than existing as a pile of loose paper memos on the corner of the desk. Those that have been read and dealt with can be deleted with a single keystroke. If a reply is needed, it can be tacked onto the message and returned to the sender; if it is for general circulation, there is an equally simple method of 'initialling' a message and sending it on.

The mail is a poor substitute for the telephone if a two-way conversation is required but how many 'phone calls really fall into this category? If there is a high likelihood that the person at the other end will not be there at the time, then the mail will often be more effective than a call. This is especially the case if you are merely conveying information or want the answer to a straightforward question, for the 'You have new mail' message will be there upon the other's return, and alert them that action is wanted. Where you need to talk to another user, a mail message requesting a call and giving times of your availability could save several missed connections both ways.

File Transfer

Some high-specification networks, like Torus Tapestry, allow you to attach any form of file - text, spreadsheet, database or diagram - to a message for mailing to other people. In MainLan you are restricted to text files within the mailing system, though it is perfectly possible to send any type via the normal file transfer utilities and use the mail to alert the recipient. Either way, being able to move files directly across the net must be more efficient than having to download files to disk before they can be given to others or, even worse, having to print out a file merely so that someone else can look at it.

Calendars and Bulletin Boards

There is more to network communications than just the mailing system. That aspect serves well for communication between individuals but the network can also be used for bringing people together into working groups. If all users have open access to at least one directory on a hard disk then you can create within it simple but effective structures for pooling ideas and information.

A calendar file can be used for arranging or announcing meetings, target dates, social activities and other special events. People could log in their own public schedules, so that others know when and where they will be; suggest tentative dates for meetings, and either include an agenda there or point to one on a bulletin board; or keep people informed of the progress of key projects. All the things that might otherwise be written onto a wallchart can be handled by a file, and more conveniently so as this can be seen without leaving the desk. You can get full-blown calendar utilities on some networks or as free-standing software and these support private and public diaries for users; but for most purposes a simple file will suffice.

On a MainLan network such a file could be easily created and updated with the Edit File utility. As this is within the network software, it is even

```
        November
        1    Monday      10.30    Design group meeting
                         noted    J.D.
                                  George
                                  Fiona
                         sorry, no Mike
        2
        3    J.D. in Scarborough for day
        4    InCom rep due p.m.
        5

        7    Monday
        8    10.00    Deadline for Polygon materials
             2.00     Polygon presentation
        9    Conf. room booked, 2 to 5 - Mike
        10   Can we meet at 1 for Xmas social planning? Fiona
                ok George
                ok J.D.
                join you at 1.30 Mike
        11
```

Figure 13.1 A networked calendar

possible to read and write on the 'calendar' in the middle of another program.

Bulletin boards are files open to anyone to read or write. On the public networks, they allow scattered users to keep in touch with one another and to spread ideas and information. We will touch on these again later when we look at external communications. On a network within a business they can be an extremely effective way of pooling knowledge in those companies that have grown too large for regular face-to-face contacts between people working in similar fields. Even in smaller companies they can serve a useful function in drawing together the ideas and findings of different individuals.

In a private network, the bulletin board will be organised as a directory on one of the shared disks. Within it there will be a set of files, each devoted to a single topic; it might be a project under consideration, a set of shortcuts and trouble-shooting tips for a software package, an agenda for a meeting, notes of comments received about the firm's products or services, or even suggestions for the annual dinner-dance. The subject matter and filename of each would be listed in an index file and if you had a problem or an interest in something of general concern you would start by checking this index to see if a relevant bulletin file existed. If there were one there, then a solution might be found by scanning the file or your own contribution may save time for someone else later. If not, then you would start a new file. For the system to work properly, each board must be maintained by one person, normally the one who first started it. It would be their responsibility to edit and organise the contributions, so that the file did not grow over-large and information remained easy to find.

```
BULLETIN FILE


Please make sure yours is listed.

NETNOTES    Network problems and solutions.         John

NEWS        Heard the latest?                       Fiona

123CUTS     Lotus tips and shortcuts.               Mike

XMASDO      Ideas wanted for Xmas party.            Sally

HARDWARE    £1500 left in the budget. Suggestions?  John

POLYGON     Project timetable.                      Fiona

WORDS       WordStar help-line.                     Sally

MARKET      What's the competition doing?           John
```

Figure 13.2 Index of bulletin files

IBM have been running a world-wide ideas pool along these lines for some years and its users have found that it can save a great deal of time by eliminating much duplicated effort. A researcher investigating the possibilities of a new product can quickly find out what other research has been done in this and related areas and may come away from the board with lists of ideas to pursue, of dead ends to avoid and of co-workers to contact.

A certain amount of frivolity and gossip may well creep into the bulletin board system, so it does need some overall supervision, but there is a good argument for encouraging its use for social interaction. Anything which helps to weld individual workers into a team will generally be for the good of the firm as a whole.

14

Going On-Line

With good modern networking software, electronic communication within the firm is so simple, friendly and reliable that most firms will be able to make effective use of it. External communications, on the other hand, are not quite as simple. The user is confronted by confusing technical jargon, complex log-on procedures, varied presentations and reliance on the quality of the public telephone lines. There are benefits to be had but you have to work a bit harder for them, and how far it is worth the effort will depend upon the nature of the business and of its existing links with the outside world.

The basic problem is one of standards. As we have already noted, network standards vary considerably but - unless someone has made some appalling buying decisions - at least they will be consistent within the firm. When you are trying to communicate with external networks and computers, the variations cannot be avoided if you want to make full use of the facilities that are available. Different systems use different speeds, protocols, commands, screen presentations and methods of organisation; users must be able to adapt their equipment and themselves to fit in with what they find at the end of the line. All have the same technical base and require the same core equipment. What follows is an attempt to present the minimum of technical information needed to be able to make effective use of communications packages.

Communications Basics

For computers to communicate via the telephone lines their signals must be converted into a suitable form by a *modem* (modulator-demodulator). There are two types of these. The audio variety send and receive signals through a microphone and speaker that connect up to a telephone handset. Once common, these are now being largely abandoned in favour of direct-wired modems that plug into the telephone wall sockets. By cutting out the conversion to and from sound, these give more reliable service. The modem can be bought either as a card to slot into the PC or as a separate box that connects to the serial port. Most will then allow you to plug the 'phone lead back into a socket on the modem, so that calls can be made normally when the computer is off-line.

For the modem to work it needs suitable communications software, which, like network software, operates at several levels. At the lowest level it handles the details of how data is passed to the modem from the computer and interpreted upon its receipt; it provides terminal emulation, making the PC's screen behave as if it were on a terminal attached to the computer at the other end of the line; it manages printing and disk filing during a communications session; and most of today's more user-friendly packages will store telephone numbers, ID's and passwords and make the connections for you.

Data Transmission

If you buy a good communications package you will generally find that it has been set up so that the main public network services can be used straight from a menu - once you have paid your subscription, that is. If your external communications will be limited to those main services, then you won't have to bother about the details of transmission protocols for they will have been written into the 'phone directory file for you. (Figure 14.1 shows part of the 'phone directory from SageSoft's Chit-Chat. Most of these entries were supplied as part of the package. You might notice the function key display at the bottom of the screen. Running operations from a single key press is much easier than having to type in commands.)

Where such connection details have not been given, or where you want to connect to a special service or a distant computer within your business,

Going On-Line

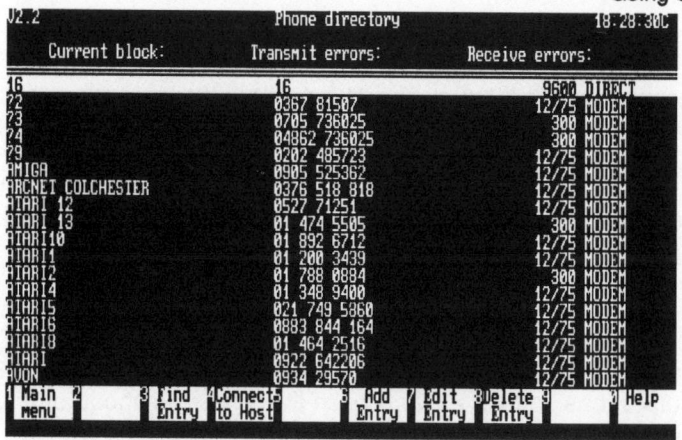

Figure 14.1 The Chit-Chat 'phone directory

then you will have to write your own directory entries. This will usually be managed via a page like that in Figure 14.2; this particular example is from Sage Chit-Chat but most communications packages work in virtually the same way.

Whoever is running the host computer will usually be able to supply you with the settings needed to make the connection, so that all you may need to do is just type them in, but a little understanding of the main features may help.

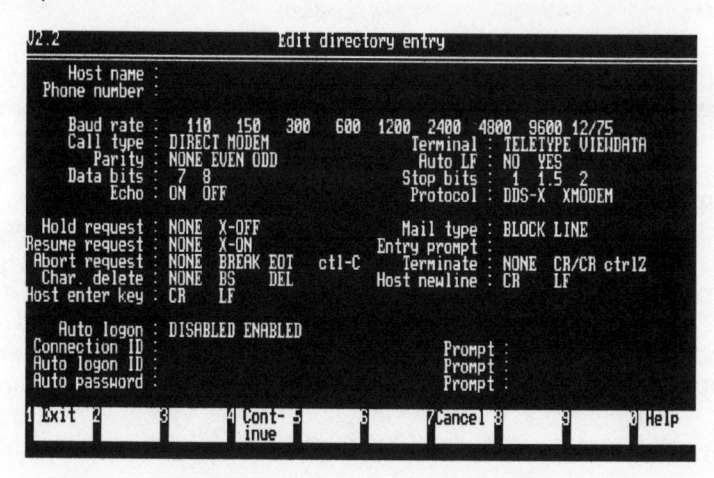

Figure 14.2 Making a directory entry

There are several alternative standard speeds and protocols for data transmission. Speed is measured by the *baud* rate - the number of bits per second - and will usually be given as two figures, representing the speed at which data is sent out by the central computer and that at which the PC replies. The slowest in common use is 300/300 baud, or a little over 40 words per second each way. Viewdata systems frequently work at 1200/75 baud, values which reflect the way the services are used. When you are communicating with a database service, most of the traffic is from the host computer (the one providing the service) to you; it will send out whole screensful of information, while you will do little more than select items from menus with single keystrokes. Some of the newer high-speed systems run at 2400/2400 but these require more sophisticated communications software to cope with the higher likelihood of errors.

Most public systems are *full-duplex*, which means that data is transmitted simultaneously both ways, though some are *half-duplex*, supporting traffic in one direction at a time only. Speed and duplex mode are combined to form the basic standards to which most modems are built:

V21	- 300 full	- suitable for most public services except Prestel;
V23	- 1200/75	- for Prestel and similar systems;
V22	- 1200 full	
V22bis	- 2400 full	- the new standards.

At the present a V21/V23 modem would be sufficient for most normal uses, but one with V22 capability could well have a longer useful life.

The speed with which data is transmitted is only part of the story. The method is equally important. Some systems use *8 Data Bits* per character, others only *7 Data Bits*, which is perfectly adequate for transmitting text files in pure ASCII form. With 7 bits you can encode any number from 0 to 127 in binary form and this range more than covers the standard ASCII characters: small and capital letters, digits, punctuation and common symbols.

Error Detection and Correction

As only 7 bits are used for identifying the character, the eighth bit is free for another purpose and that is *parity checking*. Where the system uses an Even parity check, the number of '1' bits in each byte is counted before transmission and, if there are an odd number, the eighth bit is set to '1'. When the byte reaches the other end, its '1' bits are again counted to make sure that there are an even number of them. If there are not, then the system knows that the data must have been corrupted during transmission and can request a re-transmission of the packet containing the faulty data.

Character	ASCII	Binary	1 Bits	Even	1 Bits	Odd	1 Bits
0	48	00110000	2	00110000	2	10110000	3
7	55	00110111	5	10110111	6	00110111	5
A	65	01000001	2	01000001	2	11000001	3
B	66	01000010	2	01000010	2	11000010	3
a	97	01100001	3	11100001	4	01100001	3
z	122	01111010	5	11111010	6	01100010	5

Figure 14.3 Parity checks

The parity checks may work on an odd or even basis. Either way they provide at best a rough and ready check on the quality of the transmission; any error which changed two bits of a byte would not be detected. Further, the method can only be used on ASCII text files. Programs, spreadsheet and database files, and even the normal output of many word processors use the full range of characters from 0 to 255, which are 8-bit binary numbers. Parity checking would corrupt these files, so if they are to be transmitted by modem a different method of error detection is needed.

The *Xmodem* file-transfer protocol is well established and widely used. It works by sending data in packets of 128 bytes at a time. Each packet is accompanied by a checksum - the total of the numerical values of the bytes. When received at the other end, the bytes are totalled again and compared with the checksum. If they do not match, a re-transmission is requested. It is not an absolutely foolproof system but the chances are very slim that two or more bytes will be corrupted in such a way that the numerical total remains the same. Xmodem is being gradually replaced by its newer and more sophisticated version, *Ymodem*.

Kermit is another file-transfer method in general use. As well as providing error checking, this has the useful ability of being able to package 8-bit binary files into a form that can be sent via systems that use 7-bit transmissions.

Terminal Emulation

When you link a PC to a public network service you have to play the game their way. The host computer will be an IBM, DEC or VAX mainframe and yours must behave as if it were the sort of terminal that would normally be attached to such a machine.

There is variation here, as elsewhere, but fortunately terminals are relatively simple beasts used in simple ways. With one significant exception, they only display text and generally use a plain scrolling screen, with new lines pushing the existing material up and off the screen. Likewise, only the central part of the keyboard - not the function and cursor keys - is used in on-line communications, so no problems are raised by this. This is one case where 'near enough' will often be good enough, so a communications pack that is capable of emulating the most common terminals - TELETYPE, VT100 and VT52 - will be able to produce a reasonable match in most circumstances.

The one exception is the type of terminal needed to cope with Prestel and similar viewdata systems. These have coloured graphics of a crude but effective variety and a 40- rather than the normal 80-column display. You can communicate with Prestel if your software lacks a Viewdata emulator but the screens are virtually unreadable.

Other Facilities

A *text editor* is an essential part of any communications pack. Its purpose is to create the messages to be sent by electronic mail, fax or telex (both of which can be accessed via the public networks). At their worst, text editors are very crude, slow and difficult to use; the best are almost as convenient as a proper word processor. In practice, the editors would normally be used only for short notes, with longer files being created off-line. We will return to this point later, when we look at electronic mail.

A communications pack that offers *auto-dial* will make life easier. With these, you store on disk the details of each service: transmission speeds and protocols, terminal type and, of course, the 'phone number. When you want to use that service afterwards, you simply give its name and the auto-dial routine makes the connection for you.

An extension of this is *auto-log on*. Dialling the number and setting up the link is only part of getting on-line. Once connected, you have to give your identification number or sign and, normally, a password. In some cases, the logging on procedure requires a series of other commands as well, to select the particular area that you want to work in. If your software includes an auto-log on facility, these routine inputs can be written into a text file and called up automatically as the connection is made. Some communications packs go beyond this, allowing you to automate whole sequences of commands and even set the time at which they should be performed.

Other facilities that will be found in some communications packs include the ability to divert incoming data from the screen to the printer or disk; and even the possibility of running multiple connections simultaneously.

With these, and a multi-tasking computer, you could set the communications software running at the start of the day, knowing that at predetermined times it would collect your electronic mail and store it on disk, check the latest share prices and output them to the printer and send the daily update files from your branch to the firm's head office.

Taken together, these mean that only one person needs to struggle with the technicalities; other users can get by with a far more limited grasp of how it all works. (Though it should be pointed out that any automated procedure that gives passwords must affect the security of the system. Anyone with access to the log-on files can gain access to the on-line services in your name.)

An *auto-answer* facility is essential if you want other users to be able to dial up your PC. This would be the case where workers in the field use portable machines to make contact with the main office, or where a firm has a number of branches which exchange information. If all external communications are to be run through the public network services, then auto-answer serves no useful purpose.

15

The On-line Services

Once you have connected your computer to the telephone line, you have become part of a network that stretches right across the world and the possibilities are limitless. If you know the 'phone numbers and the protocols, and have the right authorisations, your PC can communicate and share data with any other on-line computer anywhere. What's more, the cost is often surprisingly little, for many of the connections can be made through the Packet Switch Stream (PSS), a Telecom data transmission service that allows you to make national calls at local rates, and international ones at little more. It's a concept that quickens the blood of many a hacker, though the hard-headed manager will no doubt be more interested in knowing just what all this can do for his or her business. With this in mind, let's focus on what is immediately available and easy to use.

The services available over the public communications networks can be conveniently divided into three major categories: messaging, which includes electronic mail, telex and fax; viewdata, drawing information from

The On-Line Services

general and specialist databases; and consumer services, ranging from ticket booking, through home banking to betting. While some of these are provided by independent organisations, almost all can be accessed via one or other of the major networks - Telecom Gold, Prestel, One-To-One and Mercury Link. A subscription to a user group within either Telecom Gold or Prestel will often be all that is needed. Though each has it own areas of speciality, there are strong cross links between the networks.

As befits a communications business, British Telecom's Gold network is primarily concerned with messaging in its various forms but a range of other services is provided via Microlink, an independent user group operating within Gold. In practice, most users get onto Gold by subscribing to Microlink. There is little extra cost in doing it that way and some of the Microlink services can be very useful. Prestel's main focus is on the provision of information and consumer services but it too has messaging facilities. Micronet, a user group within Prestel, is the main gateway to other networks. It sometimes appears that the most significant differences between Gold and Prestel are not in what they do but in how the services are organised and presented to the users.

Prestel is a *Viewdata* system. It displays information a page at a time, using colour, large text and simple block graphics to create eye-catching screens. Pages can be accessed either by selecting from a menu with a one- or two-digit number, or by keying in the page number directly. As the main flow of data is from Prestel to you - a screenful in exchange for a key press - connections to Prestel are made at 1200/75 baud.

Telecom Gold is a *Teletype* system. Data is written onto the screen as plain text, scrolling steadily upwards, and while the displays may not be particularly attractive, at least you get a lot more information on the screen at any one time. As Gold is intended more for communications than for information provision, the flow of data is much the same in either direction. Connections to Gold are therefore usually made at 300 baud, though a 1200/75 mode is also available for when you want to use Gold to access databanks.

Electronic Mail

In essence, the public E-mail service works the same as the mail facility of an internal network. Each user has a private 'mailbox' held in a central computer, where mail can be stored until it has been read and dealt with; and messages can be sent to any other user on the system, providing their identification signs are known. Telecom Gold runs the largest and

The On-Line Services

most successful E-mail service but Prestel, Mercury Link and One-to-One are viable alternatives. Subscription charges and running costs vary but properly used electronic mail need not be expensive and can offer some useful economies.

The main difference between E-mail and mail on a network lies in the way in which it should be used, which in turn is dictated by cost considerations. The public services charge for the memory space occupied by your incoming mail and the telephone companies charge for the time you spend on-line. So, economical E-mail users who want to read their mail will copy it all down onto a disk in their PC, remove it from central storage and then hang up. The mail can then be dealt with at leisure and without incurring 'phone charges. Likewise, when sending mail to others, long messages will be prepared beforehand and stored as text files on disk. The alternative - to write them while on-line - in neither convenient nor cheap. The networks' text editors are rarely as easy to use as your favourite word-processing software and can only be used as fast as data can be transmitted down the 'phone line. (Trying to send messages at 1200/75 baud - i.e. over a Prestel connection - can be very frustrating, as even two-fingered typists can hit keys faster than the characters can be transmitted.)

All public network services have this facility to load text files to and from mailboxes but only a few of the smaller specialist networks can be used for transferring other types. Pure ASCII text files are easy to transmit. Those that use all 8 bits - programs, and data files from spreadsheets, databases and word processors - require special techniques, as we saw earlier when looking at protocols. In practice, binary files are normally only transmitted across direct links between branches of a business, or via enthusiasts' bulletin board systems.

E-mail is for business-to-business communication but only to a limited extent and not always directly. There are some practical reasons for this. Surprisingly, one is speed. Mail may not be read as regularly as it should, so a telephone call will always be more immediate, though some E-mail services do alert users when mail arrives. A second is directness. Unless the recipient has an individual mailbox within the business, the message will not land directly on the right desk in the way that a letter would; and if the second business is not an E-mail user, the message will not get through at all. There are solutions to this; in Microlink's Telemessage service, for example, the mail travels from the user through to the destination town over the networks and is then transcribed to paper and posted over the last leg. It's the equivalent of the telegram and less than half its cost.

The On-Line Services

```
MICRONET DEMO              565021119      0P
   MICRONET MAILBOX THU 20 NOV 86
   To 919993738#
      JULIA BONDS

>  Hi, Julia

   Will you be able to come
   to the party on Saturday ?

   RSVP via mailbox


   From  J J  EDWARD
         919999800

MESSAGE SENT, KEY # TO CONTINUE
```

Figure 15.1 Using E-mail

Telex

An E-mail message has no legal validity, unlike a telex or a written document, and is therefore not an ideal medium for invoices, estimates or a contract of any form. Once again, the network services have sought to meet this problem, and most offer a link through to the telex service. This can be very good value for those businesses that make only occasional use of the service and more convenient than using the local telex bureau. Individual telexes are significantly more expensive to send via Telecom Gold than they are if you are a registered telex subscriber but it requires no expensive equipment to use and there are no hefty rental charges to pay. If the purpose of a telex machine is mainly to receive them, rather than send them, then the E-mail alternative is much more economic. Incoming telexes are converted to mail and stored in your normal mailbox, at no cost apart from the usual storage charges. Some of the more sophisticated communications packages can cut down costs by storing non-urgent telexes and sending them after 8.00 pm when the service is 10% cheaper.

Where E-mail does have more direct value is within a scattered business. It may be scattered in the sense of having several branches or distant departments, or in the sense that some staff spend significant amounts of time working off-site. Rep's, field-workers and consultants may find it useful to take a portable PC out with them, whether to send back orders, request information or whatever. In these sorts of situations, firms may find the Closed User Group a useful tool. Telecom Gold, Mercury Link,

The On-Line Services

Prestel and other large networks offer group mailboxes for company use. These can be subdivided, creating separate areas for individuals and notice boards open to all members of the CUG, making communications within the group easier and more direct. (Closed User Groups also operate as clubs and specialist services within the public networks. Microlink is itself a CUG within Telecom Gold and there is a similar CUG, Micronet, within Prestel.)

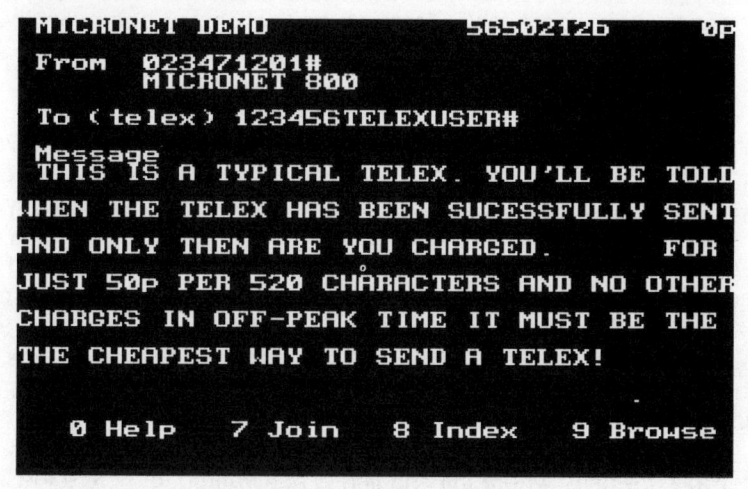

Figure 15.2 Telex the easy way

Direct Data Communications

Where there are large quantities of data flowing between distant parts of a firm, it may be more convenient and economic to bypass the public networks. An estate agent with several branches might want to send daily updates between offices so that each is aware of properties sold or new to the books of the others. A possible solution here might be to set up one central PC with an auto-answer facility and have others dial in with their update files at a fixed time each day. During that time, the central PC would be plugged in to one of the 'phone lines and left running with its communications software in host mode. This would be quite feasible with a multi-tasking machine, as it could be put to other uses at the same time. With a normal PC, it would not be able to do anything else for that half hour or so but at least it would not require anyone to look after it.

Direct data communications of this type would incur no external charges, apart from that of telephone time. Where there is a high level of usage between fixed sites, it would be worth having a special line installed by

British Telecom. This offers economies of scale and the private line should prove to be more reliable - and more secure - than the public 'phone lines.

Internetworking

Internetworking is the linking together of networks in distant offices or different businesses, sometimes by a direct line but more often by modem and 'phone. In its most sophisticated form, stations on one network can then address individual stations on the other but this is difficult - and therefore expensive - to achieve.

There are two types of connections, made via *bridges* or *gateways*. A bridge is used when both nets use the same protocols for data transmission and are identical at the physical and data link layers. Because the connection is at such a basic level, the two sets of stations can communicate as if they were part of the same network, although this can cause problems. If either network had been operating anywhere near capacity, then bridging may well push it into overload as the data then travels all the way round the linked nets. *Smart bridges* can overcome this problem by monitoring all traffic and holding back that which is not intended for the other stations.

Gateways are used where full bridging is not wanted, or where the links are between different types of network. As long as the systems are compatible at the network layer, a gateway can cope with the differences of speed and low-level data handling, allowing users to address specific remote stations. Gateways are also used to create links between the public networks; for example, a Micronet user can access the Telecom Gold services from within Prestel, via the Interlink gateway.

Internetworking is not possible with a MainLan network at present, though it would be feasible to create a connection between single stations on either net. Only that pair would be able to communicate but all file transfers and mail could be handled by them. If yours is a business in which there will be networks on two or more sites, and you will want to be able to create full links between them, then you would be best to dig deeper into your budget and standardise on one of the up-market networking systems.

Accessing the Databanks

There are enormous quantities of data at the other end of your telephone line, just waiting to be tapped. Prestel alone has over 300,000 screen pages of data, roughly equivalent to ten 500-page reference books.

Though Prestel is the largest of the on-line information services, it is not the only one. Telecom Gold and Microlink subscribers have direct access to a wide range of information services. How much of this information can be put to good purpose within your business is something that only you can judge but it is not to be ignored.

Some of the on-line data is of general interest - weather forecasts, train timetables, national news, share price summaries - and costs nothing to access, apart from the telephone charges. Most of it could be learnt equally well from the newspapers, radio, Oracle or by a 'phone call; the advantages of the database services are that the information is well organised, regularly updated and available 24 hours a day.

Specialist information is provided by CUG's within Prestel and by separate databank services. The most significant of the Prestel CUG's is CitiService SEAQ (Stock Exchange Automatic Quotation), devoted to share and commodity prices, money markets and exchange rates - an invaluable source of up to the minute information for anyone involved in share dealing. The service is available only to subscribers and is not cheap, with quarterly charges of around £40 for private and over £100 for commercial users, plus 10p per page access charge and the telephone time; but the active investor needs to be able to monitor market movements as they occur. Other forms of gambling are also catered for on Prestel via an on-line betting service run by Ladbrokes.

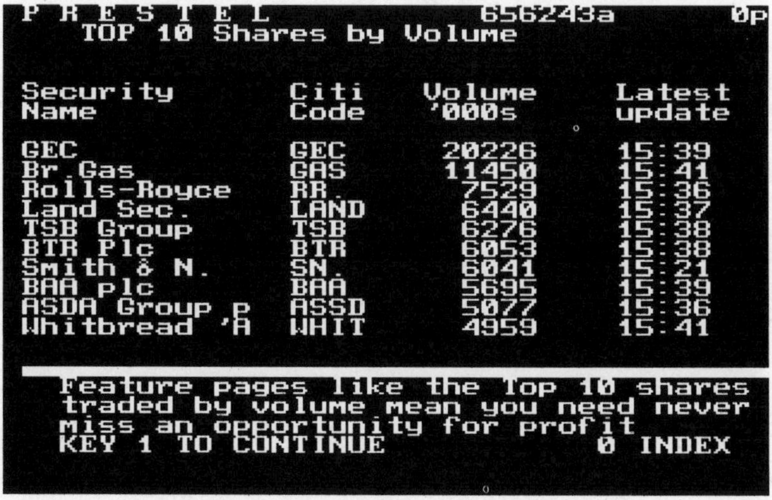
P R E S T E L 656243a 0p
TOP 10 Shares by Volume

Security Name	Citi Code	Volume '000s	Latest update
GEC	GEC	20226	15:39
Br.Gas	GAS	11450	15:41
Rolls-Royce	RR.	7529	15:36
Land Sec.	LAND	6440	15:37
TSB Group	TSB	6276	15:38
BTR Plc	BTR	6053	15:38
Smith & N.	SN.	6041	15:21
BAA plc	BAA	5695	15:39
ASDA Group p	ASSD	5077	15:36
Whitbread 'A	WHIT	4959	15:41

Feature pages like the Top 10 shares traded by volume mean you need never miss an opportunity for profit
KEY 1 TO CONTINUE 0 INDEX

Figure 15.3 Part of SEAQ's service for investors

The On-Line Services

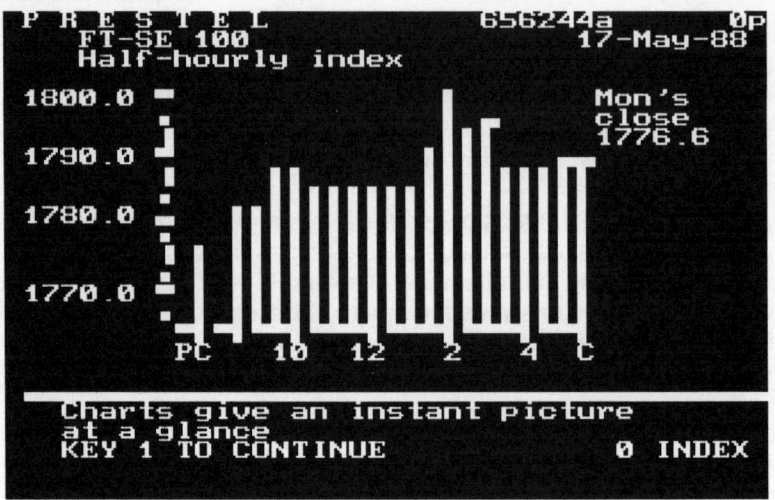

Figure 15.4 Viewdata graphics are crude but effective

A variety of specialist information services can be accessed via Telecom Gold or by direct dialling. Some are available only to subscribers, others are open to any Gold users. All charge by time, with costs ranging from 5p to £3.00 per minute, and the rates tend to reflect the value of the data. Key services for commercial users are listed below.

Infocheck and *Jordans* both provide detailed information about the financial status of UK registered companies. Ten minutes' research on these would cost around £30, but could save far more by revealing that potential customers or suppliers are not as creditworthy as they may seem.

Kompass On-line offers a similar financial status check service but also holds data on other aspects of companies such as their products, ownership, trade names and top management. Search facilities include one which allows you to create a mailing list of individuals selected by job titles from companies which meet particular criteria. This could be a very effective way of organising a mailshot aimed at commercial buyers.

Data-star, *FinTech*, *IRS Dialtech* and *IDB Online* offer a wide range of scientific and technical data, much of it focussed for the business user.

AIMSNEWS contains details of EEC and government grants and assistance for British industry.

For travellers, the *Official Airline Guide* gives schedules and rates for all the major airlines and the *Telebooking* service lets you book tickets on main line rail services to and from London.

Most of the information that is available on-line could be found from other sources but not with the same speed or convenience. The benefits will be felt most strongly by those businesses that have a regular need for up-to-date information. The services may well prove to be less economic for occasional users, for it takes practice to find your way round these large databases and the charges are clocking up all the time that you are on-line.

Other On-line Services

Prestel has been trying, since its inception, to get its on-line consumer services into general use. So far the response has been patchy largely because data communications have yet to spread beyond the bounds of the enthusiasts and the business sector.

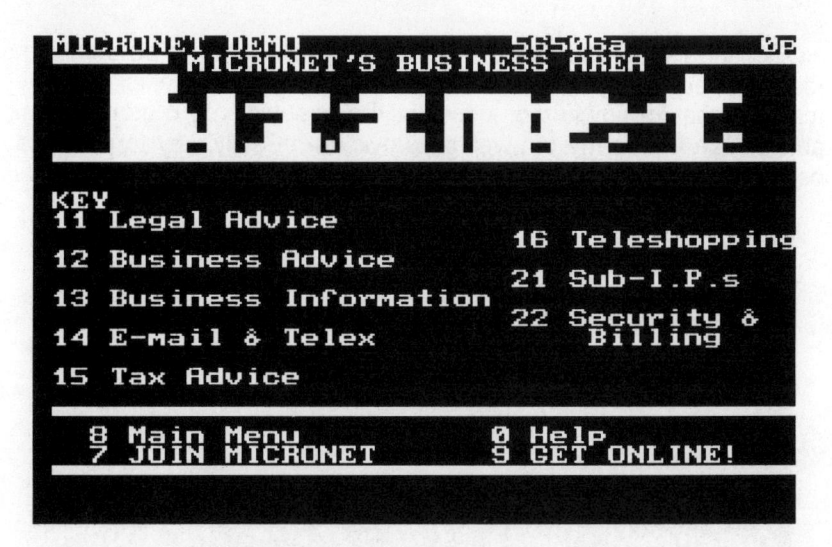

Figure 15.5 Prestel on-line services menu

Its *Teleshopping* pages have produced only limited interest from either the retail trade or the public but if your business offers a product or service relevant to on-line communications, this may be a viable selling medium.

The On-Line Services

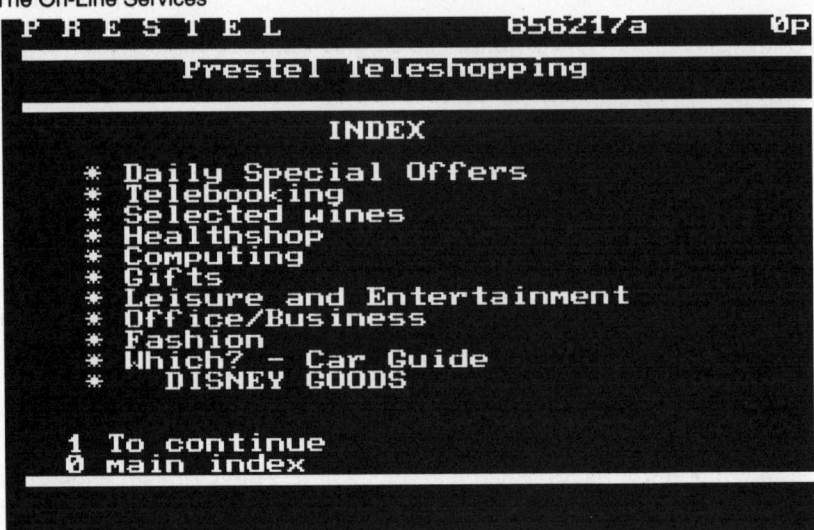

```
P R E S T E L              656217a         0p
           Prestel Teleshopping

                    INDEX
         * Daily Special Offers
         * Telebooking
         * Selected wines
         * Healthshop
         * Computing
         * Gifts
         * Leisure and Entertainment
         * Office/Business
         * Fashion
         * Which? - Car Guide
         *    DISNEY GOODS


         1 To continue
         0 main index
```

Figure 5.6 Prestel Teleshopping menu

HOBS, the Home and Office Banking Service seems to be somewhat more successful and does hold out the possibility of more efficient money management for any firm or individual that is sufficiently organised to be able to use it properly. As well as providing an easy way to pay bills - especially to other HOBS users - it also allows you to monitor your finances

```
P R E S T E L              656238a         0p
     BANK OF SCOTLAND  Account Details
        As at close of business yesterday
        Inveralder Branch

    Account No                         00428407

    Ledger Balance                       145.84
    Today's Items                       -373.27
    Fund transfers pending                 0.00
    Keycard withdrawals pending          -75.00

    Debit interest accrued                -1.12
    Charges accrued                       -0.50

    Overdraft limit                     1800.00

    Cash available from Autoteller        25.00

        Key 1 to continue
        Key 0 for main index
```

Figure 5.7 HOBS example screen

regularly and to switch cash between a deposit and a current account so that surplus balances can earn interest.

Prestel's *Legal Advice* and *Business Advice* may also be of value; while over at Telecom Gold there is an *Insurance Service*, providing on-line quotations; *Textnet*, a database of translation, writing and design services; and a *Typesetting* service that will turn coded text, from your word processor, into bromides ready for pasting up into a magazine or book.

The public network services, software houses and computer companies have been telling us for the last few years that the communications revolution is just around the corner and that soon we will all be linked by modem and 'phone. It doesn't quite seem to have happened yet, but there is no doubt that the number of people and firms going on-line is increasing steadily. At the last count, Prestel had 82,000 users, of which 50,000 are from businesses, and Telecom Gold had over 100,000 subscribers, the majority again commercial. It is a small but significant section of the business community - perhaps it's time you joined.

Appendices

A

The Multi-user Alternative

Before taking a final decision on a PC network, it is worth spending a little time on those multi-user systems that are based around high performance micros or minicomputers. There are situations where a multi-user system is a better solution than a network.

Unlike a network, where every workstation is an independent computer, a basic multi-user system will contain only a single computer, with the workstations being 'dumb' terminals. They are 'dumb' in the sense that they have no processing power, no memory and can do nothing by themselves. Data typed in at the terminal keyboard is passed directly to the central computer for processing; it can't even be displayed on the monitor without going through the central machine. More up-market systems have 'smart' terminals, with some on-board memory and capable of independent processing, and at the top of the range the distinction between multi-user system and network becomes blurred. Is it a multi-user system with intelligent terminals or a network with a high-

The Multi-user Alternative

performance machine acting as file server and network manager? At this level, the difference is less in the hardware than in the operating systems and in the way that they are used. For the rest of this appendix, we shall concentrate on those more basic systems that could be within the financial reach of smaller companies.

Sharing the processing power of one computer between a dozen or more users may seem inefficient but in practice it can work very well. The central processors in these multi-user systems are extremely powerful beasts, capable of handling far more than any mere human can throw at them in the normal course of events. You may be able to type at 100 words a minute but these processors can perform millions of operations each second.

It's worth recording that those used in the present generation of PC's are not far behind. (In fact, some of the smaller multi-user systems have the same 80386 processors that are used in the higher performance PC's.) Even the humblest PC's give few causes for complaint over their speed - and if you have to wait five seconds while it recalculates a couple of thousand sums on a spreadsheet, this is nothing compared with the time it waits while you think of what to type in next!

Multi-user systems take advantage of this discrepancy in performance, and divide the central processor's power between a set of users.

Time Sharing

The division is done on a time-share basis. The processor gives its complete attention to each terminal in turn, for a fraction of a second at a time. It will check the keyboard and empty the buffer (temporary store) of anything that has been typed since last it looked; perform a little more of any task that has been set by that terminal; and send back any output that's due. At any given moment, the central computer might have a dozen or more programs current, of which one will be actually going through the processor and the rest will be on hold, with any relevant data tucked into a portion of its large main memory. It's a juggling act, and a good processor can keep a lot of balls in the air.

The slowest part of the system is generally the transfer of data to and from the terminals but, even there, the users are rarely aware of any delay. A typical multi-user system transfers data at 9600 baud - 9600 bits, or 1200 characters, per second. With 16 terminals, it is effectively running at 600 baud (9600 / 16) for each terminal - enough to capture 75 keystrokes a

The Multi-user Alternative

second from every user. Even with a 32-terminal system, and everyone typing at once, the single processor should, in theory, be able to cope with all that is sent its way. (In practice, the systems tend to slow down when they are getting close to their limits. We'll return to this in a moment. It's also worth noticing at this point that to run a multi-user system at 9600 baud the terminals must be reasonably close to the central computer. Transmissions to and from more distant machines must be at a slower speed or data corruption becomes a problem. With the normal types of cable, 20 or 30 metres is about the limit for reliable high-speed data transfer.)

The real speed of multi-users is shown in data processing, particularly where large files are involved. Once the user has sent the instructions through from the terminal, operations are performed entirely within the central processor. As this has immediate, unrestricted access to the hard disk it can sort, update and search through files without the data transmission timelag that would be found on a PC network.

Downtime

So much for the advertisement for multi-user systems but what about the hidden catches? The major potential problem lies in the fact that the system is totally dependent upon the one central computer. If it goes down, the whole system goes down with it. No one can do any work until it has been repaired, and there's a distinct possibility that data will have been corrupted and the work done since the previous back-up will have to be redone. The firm must have a maintenance contract on the equipment, with a guaranteed fast service, and such a contract is expensive (typically 10 - 20% of the initial cost). But downtime can be even more expensive.

Compare that with a network, where the failure of a workstation will normally be no more than an inconvenience, with little impact on the rest of the network. If a hard disk, or its server, goes down it is more troublesome but still generally manageable. Data will be lost, as it would on a multi-user system, but the other stations will still be able to perform some processing. It will often be possible to transfer the work to a second hard disk and have the office functioning properly again after only a short while. A high-cost maintenance contract is less essential; it is often cheaper to replace failed equipment or call out a local repair service as needed.

Reaching the Limits

Multi-user systems have a fixed capacity. They may be designed to run 8, 16, 24 or 32 terminals but there is always a built-in limit. As this limit is approached, the whole system starts to slow down. The central processor has to spend more and more time juggling - keeping track of the demands of all its users - and less time performing useful work. The only solution is a major upgrade or the replacement of the central computer. It is worth noting that the practical limits of a multi-user system are almost always significantly below the advertised number. If the salesman claims that it can run 16 terminals, then assume that it will manage 12 well, be struggling by 14 and on the point of collapse at 16.

Networks have their limits too, though they are usually much higher than for a multi-user system in the same price bracket. As they near their limit they will slow down - but in a quite different way. The workstations will continue to process as quickly as before but the transmission of data across the network will be slower. How much impact this has on the overall efficiency of the office will depend upon the type of programs being run. It may simply mean that users have to wait ten seconds rather than two for a file to load; or it may make some operations impossibly slow.

Pricing

A multi-user system with dumb terminals will tend to cost around the same as a network of similar size and power but, because there is far less flexibility over size, there is less flexibility over price. Each system is built to take a certain number of terminals and is only really economic when it is used at or near its maximum. The main cost of the system lies in its central computer and not in the terminals, which are relatively cheap. Those with monochrome screens are typically around £300 to £500, though a good colour display could push the price over £1,000. This is quite different from a network where the cost is spread pretty evenly over all the workstations.

It seems to be in the nature of computer systems to grow, and rather quickly too. Initially, a 4-user system may appear to be all you need but the chances are that within a few months or so you will want to add more workstations as you realise that there are other operations within the business that would benefit from computerisation. So, with this in mind, let's look at the options for a firm that knows that it needs at least half a dozen terminals now and could realistically expect that number to double over the next couple of years.

The first approach is to buy for future expansion. In this particular case, the Jarogate Sprite 386 or similar would be a reasonable choice. The Sprite is a 16-user system costing around £25,000, for which you get the central machine with a 40 Mb hard disk, fast tape streamer and one master terminal. Other terminals are bought separately, and 5 with good quality monochrome monitors would add around £2,000 to the cost. At a total of £27,000, this has cost £4,500 per user - far more than you would have paid for a 6-user network. However, as the system is capable of handling up to 16 terminals, it can be expanded very cheaply up to that point. A further 6 terminals would bring the total up to about £30,000 but, spread over 12 users, this gives a more reasonable price of £2,500 per user.

The alternative approach is to buy a system which just meets the current needs and upgrade it later, but this may be neither simple nor cheap. A typical 8-user system like the Comart CP3000 costs about £18,000 - and something over £20,000 when you include half a dozen terminals. At about £3,000 per user, that is not too bad and a seventh and (possibly) eighth could be added for very little. However, you will meet a marked step-up in costs when you try to expand beyond the design capacity of the system. Before the ninth terminal can be added, you must first install an expansion board, at a cost of £3,000 or more.

Operating Systems

At present, the most common multi-user operating system is Unix, or Xenix as the IBM version is called. In its raw state it is highly unfriendly - worse than MS-DOS - with terse commands and single-letter options. In the hands of an experienced specialist it is fast and powerful, but it is difficult and confusing for occasional users. The situation is made worse by the fact that Unix is not a unitary system. Manufacturers are developing their own versions with their own improvements, so that software (and people) will not necessarily transfer from one Unix system to another without adaptation.

There are some improved front-ends now available. The best have multiple windows, easy to use menus and pop-up help screens, which all serve to make Unix much more accessible to non-specialists. It should be noted that, until recently, Unix was mainly used in large corporations, and research and academic institutions. It is only just starting to be taken up by smaller businesses and there is a limited range of commercial software that will run under Unix. Prices reflect both the scarcity and the big organisation background. With few exceptions, Unix software is more expensive than its MS-DOS equivalent.

The Multi-user Alternative

Concurrent DOS is another popular alternative. Like Unix it is both multi-tasking and multi-user, though it sets strict limits on the number of terminals. (Unix sets no limits.) If the multi-user system is based on the 80386 processor, then Concurrent DOS can cope with a maximum of 16 users. On the positive side, this system can run the many existing (single- and multi-user) applications programs written to run under either CP/M or MS-DOS, and there is a steady increase in new software designed to take advantage of the multi-tasking and multi-user facilities of Concurrent DOS.

In the Office

When a business is trying to decide between a multi-user system and a PC network it has to look very carefully at its computing needs. What sort of programs will be running for most of the time? Which applications are most important, and where is speed most important?

If you are processing the payroll or the accounts of a large company, running a mail-order business or performing any other operations on very large files, then you will do it quicker if your computer has immediate access to the hard disk where the files are stored. This is because much of the operating time is spent hunting through the disk to get the required records, and relatively little time is spent actually processing them. A stand-alone computer system has this immediate access to hard disk data, and so does the central computer of a multi-user system. It may well be dividing its time between half a dozen different tasks but the time spent on file-processing is used very efficiently.

A network cannot cope as well with the same kind of data processing. When a workstation is updating a file on a remote hard disk, each packet of data requires two transmissions across the network: the initial request and the reply from the file server. Actual transmission time is insignificant but waiting for access to the network can cause delay. The more people that are involved in the same kind of data processing, the heavier the traffic on the network and the greater the delay caused by collisions.

When you turn to other types of business computing, the balance shifts in favour of PC networks. In word processing and spreadsheeting, the files are usually relatively small; a twenty-page report takes about 50K and a spreadsheet file of the same size would be big enough to cover umpteen screens. These quantities of data can fit very easily, alongside the application program, inside a PC's memory. Once the main program and the file have been transferred across the net, the workstation will make few more demands upon the network until the work is finished.

The Multi-user Alternative

True, the more sophisticated programs are so large that they will not fit into memory in one piece. Instead, the main routines are loaded and the lesser-used routines are pulled in as overlays when they are needed. But the point is, they are the *lesser-used* routines and therefore rarely loaded. Likewise, very large reports and the accounting spreadsheets of big companies may have to be taken in a section at a time but there will be long intervals between each loading operation as the user edits the data. This is all quite different from database work, where the files are typically massive and processing requires constant access to them.

In practice, most businesses will be running a variety of applications programs. They will want to process their accounts and their payroll, send out mailshots, draw up cashflows and budget forecasts, write letters, design advertisements and brochures and all the other activities of a busy office. Whether a multi-user system or a PC network is the right solution will depend very much on the relative importance of each application. Most smaller businesses will normally find that a network gives more flexibility while coping adequately with their heaviest file-handling. A larger firm might well install a multi-user system to run its accounts or to manage a big database but this would probably exist beside a network.

Summary - Multi-User Systems and Networks

Multi-User Systems	Networks
Central processor, dumb terminals.	Independent processing power.
Central failure stops system.	Can tolerate some breakdowns.
Fast data transfer at all times; processing slows when over-used.	Fast processing at all times; data transfer slows when over-used.
Copes well with large files and heavy data processing.	Works best with files that can be fully loaded into workstations.
Restricted physical range.	Can spread over larger sites.
Expensive maintenance contracts essential.	Same day repair less vital, therefore cheaper servicing.
Cheap to expand up to limits; but limits inflexible.	More flexible in size and price.
Limited software under Unix; Concurrent DOS can run MS-DOS programs.	Plentiful MS-DOS (single-user) software; increasing multi-user.

B

The Data Protection Act

Any firm which intends to use computers to store personal information about individuals must be aware of the requirements of the Data Protection Act. This applies whether those individuals are its employees, people in other firms or members of the public at large. In essence, the Act gives people the right to know what is written about them in computer files and places an obligation upon the computer user to collect and use the information fairly and to keep it securely.

The Data Protection Registrar was appointed in 1984. The main duties of the office are:

- To establish a public register of Data Users

- To spread information about the Act and the Data Protection Principles

- To take appropriate action about any alleged breaches of the Act

Registration

Since May 1986, any individual, computer bureau or firm holding personal data on computer has been obliged to register with this office, unless they are covered by one of the exemptions.

On registering, the data user must supply descriptions of:

- The nature of the personal data being stored

- The use that will be made of it

- The sources from which the information will be taken

- The people to whom it may be disclosed, other than the subjects

- Any foreign countries to which the data may be passed

Failure to register is a criminal offence, as is misuse of data by a registered user. To date there have been no significant prosecutions, and the low number of registrations suggests that many organisations have failed to register or have decided to avoid any problems by transferring non-exempt personal data to paper files, which are not covered by the Act.

Coverage and Exemptions

The Act covers personal data, defined as information about living, identifiable individuals and including expressions of opinion about them, though not statements of intent towards them. Its main focus is such sensitive data as medical records, credit ratings and criminal history. With these, the release of information to the wrong people, or errors in the data being held, could be financially or socially damaging to the individual.

There are some clear exemptions. You do not need to register if:

- You are a home computer user, holding data only for personal use

- The subjects are members of a club and have agreed to the use of computer files

- The data is only held for the purpose of calculating wages or keeping accounts

- The data consists only of names and addresses for mailing lists

- The data is about companies, and individuals are only identified as contacts within the firms

Other situations are less clear. The distinction between expressions of opinion and statements of intent means that a file which contained '*this man is useless*' would be subject to the Act but one which said '*let's try and ease this bloke out*' would not be subject. This is obviously a rather grey area but it would be in keeping with the spirit of the Act if any data which may affect a person's future should count as falling within its scope.

The Data Protection Principles

All registered Data Users must abide by the Principles laid down in the Act. If they fail to do so they can be served with an enforcement notice, backed with the threat of criminal prosecution, or required to de-register and to cease holding personal data.

The Principles state that data must be:

- Collected and used only for those purposes described in the register entry

- Accurate and cover no more than necessary

- Deleted when no longer required for its proper purpose

- Kept securely, and not accessible to unauthorised people

As part of this, individuals have the right to know if information is held about them, can demand to see the record and can have any errors corrected or removed. If they have suffered from any misuse of data, or because the data was incorrect, they have the right to compensation.

From the point of view of the individual, it is something of a shame that this right does not extend to data stored on paper, nor to any of those government departments which hold such sway over our lives.

In Practical Terms

If you are using computers to handle the *payroll*, there is no need to register as long as the only data held is that which is needed for the calculations: name, works number, NI and tax details, rates of pay, hours worked, bonuses and similar. If there is anything else in the files - even if it is only notes about possible future roles or promotion - then your firm should be registered.

Any file used for *personnel management* must fall within the Act. It is not possible to bypass the legislation by omitting employees' names and using only reference numbers, with a linked paper file. As long as there is some means of identifying individuals, no personal data can be held on computer without registration. Courtesy and good management also demands that you should inform your employees of computerisation and of their rights under the Act.

Where the *accounts* are computerised, registration will rarely be necessary. The data held on individuals among your customers and suppliers will be unlikely to qualify as 'personal'. You may have set credit limits but this is a reflection of your business, not of the individual's credit rating.

A mail order or retail firm that kept a *database* of their customers' buying habits would fall within the scope of the Act, for it would be possible to make assumptions from that data about the individuals' financial circumstances and perhaps more personal details.

Security

If you do become a registered Data User, there will be a legal obligation to take suitable measures to ensure the security of the data, specifically:

- That data can only be accessed by authorised personnel.

- That those people only make proper use of the data.

- That proper back-ups are made so that data is recoverable in the event of failure.

The Act's recommendations about security are very sensible and worth taking on board for all of your sensitive data.

The Data Protection Act

Location of Computers and Data Storage:

- Access and sight of screens and printouts should be restricted to authorised personnel.

- Discarded printouts should be disposed of securely.

- There must be suitable precautions against theft and fire.

- Back-up copies of data must be stored separately from live files.

- If tapes or disks are re-used outside of their original area, they must be wiped to prevent old data reaching the wrong hands.

Security via Software:

- Passwords should only be known by those who need to know.

- Where possible, use multi-level passwords to restrict access to those areas with which users are actively concerned.

- Use all available checks to ensure that data is valid on entry.

Staff Management:

- Staff with access to personal data must be reliable.

- Proper training and the enforcement of disciplinary rules are essential.

- Responsibility for security should be clearly assigned.

Further Information

The Data Registrar publishes a set of well-written guides to the Act. These can be obtained free from:

Office of the Data Protection Registrar
Springfield House
Water Lane
Wilmslow
Cheshire
SK9 5AX

C

SageNet

This was the precursor of Sage MainLan and is simpler - and cheaper - than its big brother. Take a look at it for, although it is more restricted in its capabilities, it may prove to be all that is needed in some situations.

In installation, operation and use of memory, SageNet is almost identical to MainLan. In theory, it can handle file transfer and printer sharing on a network of up to 63 stations, and full multi-user applications on up to 10. In practice, you would not really want to use it on a network of more than half a dozen machines. SageNet transfers data at a lower speed - 1 Mb/s rather than 4 Mb/s - and the maximum network length is 200 metres as opposed to MainLan's 500.

The menu structure has the same basic structure as MainLan's and, for the most part, the commands are all but identical. As they have largely been covered in Chapter 5, there is no point in repeating details here. Let us then concentrate on the variations.

The *Files* and *Mail* commands are identical to those of MainLan, as are those of the *Printers* set, though this lacks a *Queue* command to allow users to check the status of the print queues. There is no *Local Print* set as such but the facilities are all available within the *Utility* set. Printing is not controlled as well here as it is in MainLan. Where a program generates printer output automatically, this will interfere with any task that the printer

SageNet

may be performing at the time. Offices using SageNet must therefore follow a much more rigorous printer discipline.

SageNet's *Security* commands are absorbed within MainLan's *Disk Share* set. And this brings us to one of the most significant differences between these two networking systems.

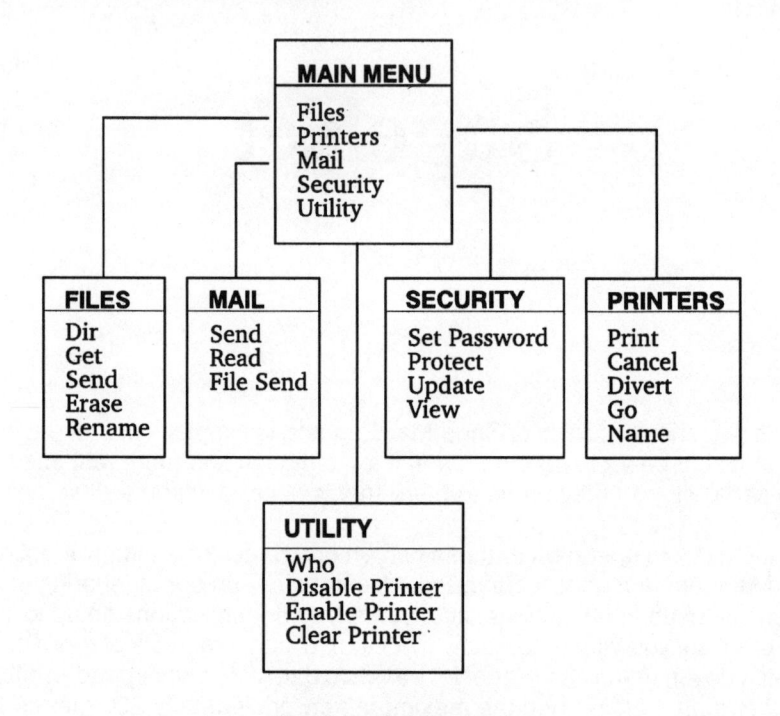

MAIN MENU
- Files
- Printers
- Mail
- Security
- Utility

FILES
- Dir
- Get
- Send
- Erase
- Rename

MAIL
- Send
- Read
- File Send

SECURITY
- Set Password
- Protect
- Update
- View

PRINTERS
- Print
- Cancel
- Divert
- Go
- Name

UTILITY
- Who
- Disable Printer
- Enable Printer
- Clear Printer

The Network Commands

With SageNet, users can transfer files from one networked disk drive to another and can arrange for some (SageSoft) programs to redirect their files to remote drives, but they cannot share disk drives in the same direct way that is possible under MainLan. The SageNet user cannot run a program that is stored on a remote drive - except by downloading it onto a local disk and then running it from there. In practice, this means that if you want to run a multi-user package under SageNet, each user must have their own copy of the program, though the data may be stored on a single drive. This is obviously a little less convenient than being able to work from one centrally-held copy but the major advantage of networking - the sharing of data - is still there.

One last point on SageNet. It was designed primarily for use with the Sage accountancy packages and it is guaranteed to work with these. With the usual provisos about ensuring the security of data files, single-user software may also be run on a SageNet system, but you would be advised to test carefully before attempting to use any multi-user software other than Sage's own.

On balance, SageNet is a viable possibility for the small office that is currently running Sage Accounts along with single-user word-processing and spreadsheet work. It provides a cheap and simple entry into networking and there is a clear upgrade path should better facilities be needed in future. The SageNet interface cards and cable are fully compatible with MainLan and the network users would have little difficulty in switching from one system to the other.

D

Tapestry II

Tapestry II has been included here as a good example of user-friendly, high-specification (if high-priced) networking software. Produced by Cambridge-based Torus Systems Ltd., Tapestry II will run on Ethernet, PC Network or Token Ring hardware, with either IBM PC's (or compatibles) or IBM PS/2 computers. The system transfers data at a fast 10 Mb/s, and can cope with up to 30 workstations spread over a maximum of 200 metres in any one segment, where stations are connected by thin Ethernet cable. These bald figures rather understate the maximum size of a Tapestry network, for thick Ethernet cable will increase the range and number of stations by a factor of three, and up to five segments can be joined into a single working net. The true maxima are therefore 500 workstations spread over 2.5 kilometres, and long-distance users can have full access to the network via special remote links.

Each Tapestry segment, or *domain*, is under the control of one manager station. All configuration is performed from this one machine, which may prove to be a limitation in a small and flexible office but becomes a more valuable feature in bigger offices. As very large networks can be difficult to manage, Tapestry II allows them to be split into linked domains, each separately controlled but with full interconnections.

Tapestry II

Tapestry II is a very powerful piece of software but one that has been designed to be user-friendly. One of the most obvious aspects of this is the use of icons for selecting functions and operations. Many new users seem to find that the graphics symbols make it easier to remember what things do, so training time can be reduced. (More experienced users - who may regard icons as a waste of screen space - can suppress this display and work from a simple menu instead.) A lot of thought has clearly gone into the screen presentations, with the aim of providing all the relevant information that may be needed for an operation, and an extensive set of Help screens does away with the need to keep chasing the manual all over the office. Control is either by keyboard or mouse; the mouse must be used for some of the screen display controls, which can prove a limitation on crowded desks.

Tapestry II offers the same facilities as MainLan - and more. The electronic mail, printing and disk-sharing routines are very similar, though Tapestry has a more flexible set of password protection and access-restriction mechanisms, so that Read and Write permissions can be set for files or directories without resort to the MS-DOS `ATTRIB` command. Larger offices may well appreciate the additional Time Management facilities that allow users to maintain diaries on the network. These are essentially private, though sufficiently open to other users for meetings to be set up across the network.

Internetworking and full external communications are possible via additional Gateway software and hardware - something that is not possible with MainLan, where computers can only establish external links on an individual basis.

These extra facilities come at a cost. To set up a Tapestry network you will need a Manager Pack at £695 (1988 prices), an Extension Pack for each station at £375 (slightly cheaper by the bunch) and an Ethernet Adaptor for every computer on the network at £395 each, plus the cable. The total netware costs for a 6-station set-up would then be around £4,800 as opposed to £1,200 for a MainLan network. The difference is enough to buy a new high-performance 386 computer or six ordinary PC's. Remote links, to bring long-distance users into the network, cost £350 for each user plus £395 at the network end.

On balance, Tapestry is to be recommended in those larger businesses that will be running networks of 30 or more stations - where the higher data transfer rates and domain-management aspects will be of value - or in those situations where internetworking, remote links or other external communications are required.

E

Product Suppliers

Amstrad plc
PO Box 462
Brentwood
Essex
CM14 4EF
Low cost computers, netware, software

Ashton Tate UK Ltd
1 Bath Road
Maidenhead
Berkshire
SL6 4UH
dBase and other software

British Olivetti Ltd
FREEPOST
London
SW15 2BR
Mid-price, good quality computers

Product Suppliers

Brother International
Shepley Street
Audenshaw
Manchester
M34 5JD
Computers and printers

Canon UK Ltd
Canon House
Manor Road
Wallington
Surrey
SM6 0AJ
Laser and other printers

Compact Software Ltd
Woodside House
Woodside Road
Eastleigh
Hants
SO5 4ET
Accounts and payroll software

Dell Computer Corporation
FREEPOST RG1462
Bracknell
Berkshire
RG12 1BR
High value 286 and 386 micros

Epson (UK) Ltd
FREEPOST TK984
Brentford
Middlesex
TW8 8BR
THE printer people

Equinet Computers Ltd
114/116 Curtain Road
London EC2A 3AH
Netware

Everex Systems UK Ltd
72 Capital Way
Edgeware Road
Colindale
London
NW9 0EW
Tape streamers

IBM UK Ltd
FREEPOST
389 Chiswick High Road
London
W4 5BR
Everything you need - at a price

InterQuadram Ltd
653/654 Ajax Avenue
Slough
Berkshire
SL1 4BG
Low cost fax and expansion boards

Level V Distribution Ltd
Ashford House
Dale Road South
Darley Dale
Matlock
Derbyshire
DE4 2EU
Xenix software specialists

MAP
107 Windsor Road
Oldham
OL8 1RP
Accounting and network software

Megatech
111-113 Wandsworth High Street
Wandsworth
London
SW18 4HY
TAS accounting and database software

Product Suppliers

Micro Peripherals Ltd
Unit 3
Wade Road
Basingstoke
Hants
RG24 0NE
Dot matrix printers

Omicron Management Software Ltd
3 Crawford Place
London
W1H 1JB
Unix, Xenix and DOS software

Opus Technology Ltd
53 Ormside Way
Holmethorpe Industrial Estate
Redhill
Surrey
RH1 2LW
Low cost PC to 386 computers

PC Communications Ltd
Elmsdale House
The Green
West Drayton
Middlesex
UB7 7PN
Communications hardware and software

Qume
Park Way
Newbury
Berkshire
RG13 1EE
Laser and other printers

R & D Technology Ltd
226 Munster Road
Fulham
London
SW6 6AZ
Netware

SageSoft Ltd
NE1 House
Regent Centre
Newcastle-upon-Tyne
NE3 3DS
MainLan, SageNet, Accounts and other software

Schneider Computers Ltd
Schneider House
5 Harrowden Road
Brackmills
Northampton
NN4 0HW
Compact PC's and AT compatibles

Semaphore Systems Ltd
7 Moreland Court
Finchley Road
London
NW2 2PJ
Expansion cards

Sentinel Software
Wellington House
New Zealand Avenue
Walton-on-Thames
Surrey
KT12 1PY
Word Perfect and other software

SoftKlone (UK)
PO Box 42
Fishponds
Bristol
BS16 4BA
Mirror II communications software

Star Micronics UK Ltd
Craven House
40 Uxbridge Road
Ealing
London
W5 2BS
Low cost printers

Product Suppliers

Torus Systems Ltd
Science Park
Milton Road
Cambridge
CB4 4GZ
Tapestry network software

Glossary

ASCII   American Standard Code for Information Interchange. Numbers which represent letters, digits and other common characters. An ASCII text file is probably the simplest form in which to transmit data.

Bandwidth   Range of frequencies used within a channel.

Baseband signals   Those transmitted in their original, unmodulated form.

Batch processing   Alterations to a master file are written into a temporary update file, which is then merged in a single process. The technique is generally reserved for use on mainframe systems and WAN's. Contrast with *interactive processing*.

Baud rate   Measurement of data transmission, in bits per second.

bps or **b/s**   Bits per second.

Bridge   Device for connecting two networks of identical type.

Glossary

Broadband signals   Used on co-axial cable systems. Signals are modulated and transmitted at a specific frequency, so that several signals can be handled simultaneously within a single cable.

Bus   Path for electrical signals. A network with a bus topology has its stations linked in a continuous line.

CP/M   Control Program for Microprocessors. The first widely accepted operating system for microcomputers, and still in limited use.

CSMA/CD   Carrier Sense Multiple Access Collision Detection. Method of dealing with data collisions on networks. Stations listen for quiet period on the carrier wave before attempting to send data.

Centralised network   One where all processing is carried out in one central computer. A multi-user system.

Co-axial   Type of cable used for TV transmissions and for high performance networks.

Connectivity   The ability of devices to communicate with each other.

DOS   Disk Operating System. Controls the keyboard, screen, memory and disk drives at the most basic level. Microsoft's MS-DOS is the one most commonly used in PC's.

Daisy chain   Type of bus topology, where the network is formed by separate loops of cable linking pairs of computers.

Database   Collection of related files, all of which can be accessed and used via the same applications program.

Data communications   Transmission and reception of computer data over a local or wide area network.

Data file   Body of information created by and used by a program, as opposed to a program file.

Data management system   Software package which allows users to create, edit, and draw information from data files organised to their own design.

Dedicated server   Computer whose processing power is used solely for managing a hard disk or printer and that cannot be used as a workstation.

Distributed network   One where many or all computers on the network are capable of independent processing.

Download   Transfer of file from a remote computer to one's own.

EPABX   Electronic Private Automated Branch Exchange. Telephonic switching system sometimes used for computer networks.

Electronic mail   Method of sending messages between computers, usually via a mailbox in a central machine.

Ethernet   Cabling system for bus-type network.

Fibre optics   Transmission of data as light signals. Used where high speed and very high performance needed.

Flow control   Regulation of transmission speeds where data is being passed between different networks.

Gateway   Device for connecting networks of different types.

IEEE   Institute of Electronic and Electrical Engineers. Its 802 committee is responsible for establishing networking standards.

ISO/OSI   International Standards Organisation, Open Systems Interface. Model providing conceptual basis for setting networking standards.

Interactive processing   Editing data file directly, one record at a time.

Interface card   Device interpreting signals between a computer and the network.

LAN   Local Area Network.

Local   Where you are, as opposed to remote.

Mainframe computer   Big job, used where massive data storage and high-speed processing essential.

Menu Display of options. With a menu-driven program you do not have to remember what the commands are, only what they will do.

Microcomputer Self-contained computer, used as a stand-alone or on a network. The most powerful approach minicomputers in performance.

Minicomputer Fitting between micros and mainframes, generally used as the basis of a small multi-user system.

Modem Device for converting computer data into telephone signals and vice versa.

Netware Software for managing a network.

Node Strictly, a junction on a network. Generally used to refer to a networked computer.

On-line Connected to a distant computer.

Operating system   see *DOS*.

Packet switching Method of transmitting data where each set of bytes is packaged with the addresses of the sender and recipient.

Peripheral Any device attached to a computer, e.g. hard disks, printers, modems and mice.

Personal computer (PC) Alternative name for *microcomputer*.

Protocol Set of rules for transmitting data.

RAM Random Access Memory. Chips for internal data storage. Data held there can be read or written much quicker than on a disk but is lost when the computer is turned off.

Remote Distant computer on a network.

Repeater Device for boosting a signal so that data can be carried over a greater distance.

Ring Type of network where the cable joining the computers forms a continuous loop.

ROM Read Only Memory. Data stored in ROM chips cannot be altered but is there permanently. Used for operating systems and some software. Programs on ROM are instantly available on start up.

Session Active connection between two computers.

Software Programs, as distinct from *hardware*, which is the equipment.

Star Type of network where stations are all joined at a single central switching box or computer.

Station Short for *workstation*.

Tap Cable leading off from main cable of bus-type network.

Teletype Display mode used for data communications. Can handle text only, and prints one line at a time with screen scrolling steadily upwards.

Terminal Keyboard and VDU attached to mini- or mainframe computer.

Terminal emulator Software which makes computer behave like a terminal. Used in communications with public networks and mainframes.

Text editor Simple word-processing software.

Token Signal used in token-passing systems to control access to the network.

Twisted pair Type of cable, normally consisting of two pairs of wires. The twisting improves their electrical properties.

Upload Transmission of file from your computer to a remote one.

VDU Visual Display Unit. Strictly speaking only the monitor but often used to refer to a dumb terminal, which consists of little more than a screen and keyboard.

Viewdata Display mode used in data communications. Each screen is printed in full, using colour and simple block graphics as well as text.

Workstation Computer available for processing work. It may have server functions but is not a dedicated server.

Index

Accounting systems, 122
AIMSNEWS, 150
Amstrad network, 30
Applications Programs,
 analysis, 71
ATTRIB for protection, 55
Auto-log on, 140
Auto-answer, 141
Auto-dial, 140
AUTOEXEC.BAT files, 50

Back-up routines, 109
Back-up systems, 85
Baseband, 31
Baud rate, 138
Bin-fodder, avoidance of, 111
Boilerplates, 124
Bridges, 148
Broadband, 32
Bulletin board files, 132
Bus topology, 32
Business Advice service, 153

Cables, 37
Cabling up, 104
Calendar file, 131
Carrier signal, 40
Cheapernet, 30

Chit-Chat, comms pack, 136
Clipper, 121
Closed User Group, 146
Co-axial cable, 38
Collision Avoidance, 41
Collision Detection, 40
Collision management, 40
Communications software, 136
Communications, external, 130
Communications, internal, 135
Communications, standards, 135
Copyright, 103
Crash, recovery from, 110
CSMA/CA, 41
CSMA/CD, 40
CUG, 147

Daisy chain topology, 33
Data bits 7 or 8, 138
Data collisions, 31
Data communications, direct, 147
Data integrity, 103
Data packets, 40
Data storage requirements, 77
Data transmission, 136
Data-star, information
 service, 150
Databanks, 148

Index

Database management
 systems, 121
dBase III, 121
dBFast compiler, 121
Deadly embrace, 118
Dedicated file server, 27, 83
Default settings, 102
Directory structure, 57
Disk Share commands,
 MainLan, 56

E-mail, economic usage, 145
Electronic mail services, 144
EPBAX, 35
Error detection in
 communications, 138
Ethernet, 30
Excel, 123
External communications, 135

File commands, MainLan, 54
File locking, 117
File server management, 107
File transfer, 131
FinTech information service, 150
Foxbase, 121
Full-duplex, 138

Gateways, 148

Half-duplex, 138
Hardware, potential
 economies, 25
Hidden costs, 26
HOBS, 152
Home and Office Banking
 Service, 152
Host computer, 140

IDB On-line information
 service, 150
Ideas pool, 133
IEEE, 43
IEEE Standards, 46

Infocheck, 150
Information services,
 specialised, 150
Insurance Service, 153
Internal communications, 130
International Standards
 Organisation, 43
Internetworking, 148
IRS Dialtech information
 service, 150
ISO, 43

Jordans information service, 150

Kermit, 139
Kompass On-line service, 150

LAN, 14
Lancia chip, 31
Legal Advice service, 153
Local Area Network, 14
Local Print commands,
 MainLan, 61
Locking, file and record, 117
Logging on procedures, 141
Lotus 1-2-3, 122

Mail commands, MainLan, 62
MainLan, 49
Memory resident, 51
Mercury Link, 144
Microlink, 144
Micronet, 144
Modem, 136
Multiplan, 123

NETBIOS, 45
NETBIOS System, 52
Netware, 16
Netware functions, 51
Network breakdown, 106
Network manager, 96
Network practices, 112
Network services, public, 136

Index

Novell Netware, 30

Official Airline Guide, 151
Omninet, 30
On-line information services, 149
On-line services, 151
One-to-One, 144
Open Systems Interconnect, 43
Optic fibre cable, 39
OS/2 operating system, 82
OSI Model, 44

Packet Switch Stream, 143
Parity checking, 138
Parity, odd and even, 139
Password protection, 108
Passwords, MainLan, 57
PC Network, 30
PC Planner, 123
Prestel, 144
Print queue, 61
Print server management, 110
Print server requirements, 76
Printer commands, MainLan, 60
Printer problems, 111
Processor types, 82
Protecting files, 55
Protocols, 31
PSS, 143

Quattro, 123

Record locking, 117
Redirectors, 59
Redundancy, 89
Reliability, 88
Retrieve, 122
Ring topology, 33
RS232 system, 44

SEAQ, 149
Security, 107
Server / Workstations, 84
Shielded twisted pair, 104

SNA, 30
Spreadsheets, 122
Star topology, 35
Stock Exchange Automatic
  Quotation, 149
SuperCalc, 123
Systems Network
  Architecture, 30

Tape streamer, 85
Telebooking, 151
Telecom Gold, 144
Telemessage service, 145
Teleshopping, 151
Teletype, 140
Telex, 146
Terminal emulation, 140
Text editor, 140
Textnet on-line service, 153
Time Domain Reflectometry, 106
Token Bus Systems, 46
Token-passing, 41
Token ring, 35
Topology, 32
Traffic, 31
Transceiver, 32
Trouble-shooting, 105
Twisted pair cable, 37
Typesetting on-line service, 153
Typical costings, 89

User training, 104
Utility commands, MainLan, 63

Viewdata emulator, 140
Viewdata systems, 138
Volkswriter, 125
VT100 terminal, 140
VT52 terminal, 140
V21/V23 modems, 138

WAN, 13
Wide Area Network, 13
Word, 124

Index

Word processing, 123
Word Perfect, 125
WordStar, 125
Workstation requirements, 74
Xmodem file-transfer
   protocol, 139

Ymodem file-transfer
   protocol, 139